FAITH THAT WOULD NOT BREAK

NOT BREAK

Part One: When the Dust Settles

Jean Joseph

ISBN'S:
Ebook: 978-1-970853-40-7
Paperback: 978-1-970853-41-4
Hardcover: 978-1-970853-42-1
Publisher: Jean Joseph

Cover design by: Jean Joseph

Scripture quotations are taken from the **New International Version (NIV)** of the Bible. Copyright © 1973, 1978, 1984, 2011 by Biblica, Inc. Used by permission. All rights reserved worldwide.

This book is a work of nonfiction. Names, characters, and events are used to illustrate lessons and experiences; any resemblance to actual persons, living or dead, is coincidental except where noted.

First Edition
February 2026

DEDICATION

This book is dedicated to the memory of my grandmother, Adecia Saintville, whose love, prayers, and faith planted seeds that continue to shape my life, even in her absence.

To those who have ever faced a season of silence, uncertainty, or struggle, this book is for you.

To the quiet warriors, the faithful waiters, the dreamers who keep stepping when no one sees, may you know that your endurance is shaping you for a purpose greater than you can yet imagine.

And to God, whose faithfulness has carried every step, who shapes hearts in ways no human hand can, and who transforms trials into testimonies, this work is a humble reflection of Your guidance, provision, and unwavering presence.

ACKNOWLEDGMENTS

I would like to begin by thanking my wife, Keziah Joseph, whose love, patience, and unwavering support sustained me through seasons when this journey felt heavy. Your faith in me never wavered, even when mine was being tested.

I am deeply grateful to my mother, Marie Bazelais, whose prayers, strength, and sacrifices laid the foundation of faith and resilience in my life long before I understood their significance.

To my children, Alana Joseph, Windy Joseph, Andre Sutton, and Adelcia Joseph, this book is part of the legacy I hope to leave you. I wrote these pages so you would understand the mission God placed on my life, the sacrifices that sometimes come with obedience, and the love that stands behind every step of this journey.

I also want to thank my brothers, Jean Toussaint and Vladimir Bazelais, and my sisters, Rose Sainvil and Dolores Murat, for their encouragement, understanding, and continued presence throughout this journey.

I would like to express heartfelt gratitude to Yolene Opont, whose constant encouragement, faith, and support have made her a sister in every way that truly matters.

I am thankful for Colorado Christian University, whose faith-centered academic environment played an important role in shaping my spiritual growth and deepening my understanding of what it means to live as a Christian.

I also extend my sincere thanks to Jeanette Doyal for her support and encouragement.

Above all, I give thanks to God, whose calling, guidance, and grace made this work possible.

PREFACE

Every journey has a beginning, but few reveal their true purpose without testing the heart, the spirit, and the mind. This book is not just a story of vision, perseverance, or the fulfillment of a promise, it is a testimony to the process that shapes us into who we were created to be.

The pages that follow were written from seasons of silence, nights of wrestling, and moments when fear threatened to define the path. They carry the lessons learned not in moments of applause, but in the quiet, unseen spaces where endurance is built, faith is tested, and character is forged.

My hope for this book is simple: that it will serve as a companion for anyone walking a path that feels too long, too heavy, or too uncertain. That it will remind you that the process is purposeful, that struggles are refining, and that the journey is always preparing you for the promise that lies ahead.

This is more than a reflection on a personal journey, it is an invitation to see the weight you carry not as a burden, but as preparation. To recognize that every delay, every trial, and every season of waiting is shaping you into the person capable of stewarding what is coming.

May the truths in these pages encourage you, challenge you, and give you the courage to step into your calling with conviction, faith, and quiet confidence.

AUTHOR'S NOTE

This book was not written to persuade, impress, or argue a point. It was written to bear witness to a calling that unfolded over time, often without clarity, certainty, or comfort. For many years, the vision that shaped these pages lived quietly within me, growing through experience, struggle, faith, and obedience. I did not always understand where the journey would lead, nor did I always know how the pieces would come together. What I did know was that the call itself never left.

The story you are about to read is not a claim of spiritual strength or personal accomplishment. It is a testimony of learning to walk forward without seeing the full path, trusting God one step at a time.

This book is written for those who have felt called to something larger than themselves but have struggled to understand how it could ever be fulfilled.

I do not present this work as a finished answer, but as an honest record of faith in motion.

CONTENTS

CHAPTER 1

THE BEGINNING

I was born in the Caribbean, on a small island wrapped in beauty and hardship, where the sun painted the mornings gold and the nights carried the quiet sound of struggle. The breeze that moved through the coconut trees always felt warm, but the lessons of life were often cold and unforgiving. From the outside, everything looked peaceful. Yet behind the walls of many homes, including mine, a silent battle was being fought every single day.

I was still a young boy when I first felt the weight of life press against my shoulders. While other children woke up thinking about games and adventure, I woke up thinking about whether there would be enough to eat that day. My earliest memories are not of toys or carefree days. They are memories of watching my father fight to keep us alive. I remember hearing his footsteps long before the sun rose, the front door opening quietly so he would not wake us. I would peek through the cracked wooden doorframe and watch him walk into the darkness, shoulders squared, his face set with determination.

He always moved with purpose, even when he was tired. His hands were rough from labor, his clothes worn from long days, and his eyes carried weight he tried his best to hide. He would often come home so depleted that exhaustion was all he had to show for the day. Days when silence spoke louder than any words he could find. Yet even when we sat around a table with empty plates and heavy hearts, he would look at us with faith in his eyes and say, "Everything will be alright." And even though I could see the struggle behind his words, I believed him, because his strength was the only stability I knew.

Many nights, I went to bed without food. Hunger is not just the absence of food. Hunger is the presence of fear. It follows you into sleep and wakes you before dawn. It is the sound of silence where laughter should be. I remember lying on a thin mattress, staring at the ceiling, whispering words that sounded like thoughts but were really prayers. I would tell myself, one day I will change this. One day I will help my family. One day I will make my father rest. I did not know how or when, but something inside me refused to accept that struggle would be my story forever.

Those nights shaped me. They taught me discipline, resilience, responsibility, and strength. They taught me that comfort does not build character; hardship does. They taught me that a man is not measured by what he owns. A man is measured by what he survives. My father survived more than I could ever fully understand, and he became my hero without trying to be. He became my example without giving speeches. His life taught me how to endure. His sacrifice taught me how to fight. His courage was not loud or dramatic. It was consistent. It was the courage of a man who keeps showing up when life gives him every reason to quit.

But not every childhood memory was formed around quiet survival. Some were formed around pain so sharp it cut into my soul and never fully healed. I was only six years old when the moment that changed my life forever occurred. My cousin, who was ten years older than me, lived with us. He was more than family. He was my protector, my role model, the person I admired most in the world. I followed him everywhere. I watched the way he walked, the way he talked, and the way people respected him. I wanted to grow up and be just like him.

Then one day, without warning, he was gone. Not gone in the way children imagine someone leaving, but gone in the way death steals breath and leaves silence in its place. I can still hear the screams, high-pitched and hollow, cutting through the air like a knife. I can still see people collapsing, bodies trembling with grief. I can still feel my legs refusing to move and my voice refusing to form words. At six years old, I learned that death does not knock. It breaks down the door and takes what it wants.

The house that once felt full suddenly felt unbearably empty. The laughter that echoed through the rooms was replaced by sobbing so heavy it made the walls feel like they were closing in. I watched the strongest adults I knew collapse under heartbreak. I watched my father stand in silence, staring into nothingness, jaw clenched, eyes filled with a storm he could not stop. That day carved a wound in me. Even now, I miss him, I wonder what he might have become, I feel the echo of that loss.

I did not understand why things like that happened. I did not understand why good people suffer or why life can change so quickly. But something changed inside me that day. Childhood innocence shattered, and a heavier awareness took its place. I began to see that life is fragile, time is not guaranteed, and purpose matters. And just when the weight felt too heavy for a child to carry, God stepped into my story in a way I will never forget.

One night, not long after losing my cousin, I had a dream so real it felt more like an encounter than sleep. In the dream, I was running, running faster than I had ever run in my life, toward a bright light filled with warmth and peace I had never known. The closer I got, the stronger the presence became. Love surrounded me like air. Power pressed against me like wind. Then I saw Him. Even though His face shone with glory, I knew instantly it was God. I ran toward Him with everything inside me, desperate to reach Him, desperate to find rest from the pain in my chest.

Just as I stretched out my hand to touch Him, He lifted His hand and stopped me. His voice filled the atmosphere, powerful yet overflowing with love. He looked into my soul and said, "Where are you going? Go back. It is not your time. I am not done with you yet."

Those words struck me like lightning. They went through me and shook me to my core. I woke up sitting straight up in the dark, breathing hard, my heart pounding like a drum. I could not move. I could not speak. All I could do was tremble, knowing without doubt that I had encountered God.

Years later, I would read words that described what I experienced before I even knew Scripture. "Before I formed you in the womb I knew you, before you were born, I set you apart," says Jeremiah 1:5 (NIV). I did not know that verse as a child, but I lived its truth. God knew me long before I knew Him. He protected me before I knew I needed protection. He kept me alive because He had already written purpose into my life.

That night became a turning point. It was the beginning of surrender. It was the beginning of transformation. I began to realize that purpose is not something we chase in the world. Purpose is something God writes inside us before we take our first breath. And no matter how dark life becomes, purpose cannot be destroyed.

After that dream, I did not suddenly become fearless or confident. I was still a child living in a world that demanded maturity far too early. But something internal had shifted. Fear no longer had the final word, and pain no longer defined my future. Even when life remained difficult, the knowledge that God had spoken to me became an anchor. I carried that moment quietly, not knowing who to tell or how to explain it, but knowing it was real. It was not something I could forget. It lived in me, shaping how I faced each day.

He did not remove hardship from my life. He did not soften every blow or explain every loss. Instead, He strengthened something deeper than circumstance. I learned early that faith does not always change what surrounds you, but it always changes what is forming within you. Even when food was scarce and grief lingered, there was a growing sense that my life was being preserved intentionally.

Every time I woke up, endured another day, or found the strength to keep going, it felt like confirmation that God's words still stood: "It is not your time." Those words did not mean life would be easy. They meant life would be purposeful. They meant my story carried weight, direction, and responsibility.

I saw strength that did not look impressive but proved enduring. I learned that faith often looks like persistence rather than celebration. It looks like continuing when there is no applause, no recognition, and no guarantee of change. That environment shaped my understanding of God long before I knew how to articulate it. God was not distant. He was present in the endurance of ordinary people doing what was necessary to survive.

As I grew older, the memory of my cousin remained close to my heart. His absence became a reminder that life is not promised in length, only in purpose. I did not understand why he was taken while I remained, but I knew I could not waste the breath I had been given. Loss taught me urgency, not panic, but intentionality. It taught me that love does not end when someone leaves this world. It becomes a responsibility carried by those who remain.

That awareness began shaping how I viewed my future. I did not dream of comfort. I dreamed of meaning. I did not imagine ease. I imagined impact. Even as a child, I sensed that my life would involve difficulty, not because God desired suffering, but because suffering would shape the strength my calling required. I could not name that calling yet, but I could feel its weight.

Faith, for me, did not begin in a church building. It began in hunger, loss, prayers whispered into darkness, and a dream that interrupted death itself. It began with the realization that God was not waiting for me to become strong before He spoke. He spoke while I was weak. He claimed me before I understood Him. He preserved me before I knew what preservation meant.

That understanding stayed with me as the idea of leaving my home began to surface. I did not see departure as abandonment. I saw it as transition. Even though fear accompanied the thought of leaving, I sensed that God was widening my world, not removing my roots. What felt like separation would later become expansion. What felt like loss would become preparation.

I wanted to understand why God had kept me alive. I wanted to honor my cousin. I wanted to honor my father. I wanted to honor God. Something shifted in me. I stopped seeing life as something to survive and began seeing it as something to steward. I did not know what God had planned, but I knew my life would not end where it started. I began to sense, deep in my spirit, that God was preparing a journey far beyond the shores of the island where I was born.

I began to see the world through different eyes. Even though I was still a boy, something in my spirit woke up. While other children laughed and chased each other through dusty roads, I found myself quieter, thinking deeper and watching more closely.

Later, I would understand what Romans 8:28 says: "In all things God works for the good of those who love Him, who have been called according to His purpose" (NIV). Back then, I could not explain it, but I could feel it. God was working through what I did not understand. He was shaping me through what looked like loss and building something inside me through what felt like breaking.

As time went on, everything around me began to feel temporary. The home that once felt permanent started to feel like a starting point rather than an ending. I could not explain it, but I sensed change coming. It felt as though God was loosening my grip on what was familiar and stretching my vision beyond what I could see. I began to understand that who I was in that season was not who I would remain.

When the time to leave drew near, the atmosphere around me shifted. People spoke about opportunity and a better future. They smiled as if the path ahead was guaranteed to be bright. Inside me, excitement was tightly mixed with fear. I was leaving everything familiar behind and stepping into a new world without knowing what waited on the other side.

In those final days, I paid closer attention to everything. I noticed the worn chairs, the marks on the walls, the rhythm of neighbors calling across the road, children running barefoot through the dust, the smell of earth after rain, and the warm evenings beneath a sky filled with stars. I wanted to remember it all. My grandmother cooked more meals than usual, feeding not only my body but my spirit. My aunt stayed close, laughing louder than normal, as if fighting the growing silence. My father worked harder, leaving early and returning late, because in our culture emotions were dangerous and strength was survival.

The night before I left, my grandmother held my hands and prayed over me. Her voice shook as she asked God to guide every step I took, surround me with protection, and never let me forget who I was. She prayed as if she were sending me into battle, and in a way, she was. Tears fell onto my hands. I cried too, quietly, trying not to make a sound. My father turned away so I would not see him wipe his face. That was his language. Quiet love. Quiet pain. Quiet strength.

When morning came, it came too quickly. My luggage was small, but my heart was heavy. My grandmother held my face gently between her hands, her eyes full of love and unspoken fear. My aunt hugged me tightly and whispered encouragement. My father stood nearby, silent, eyes fixed on the ground, carrying love, fear, and grief all at once. As I stepped toward the vehicle, each step felt heavier than the last. I turned one final time to look at the home that raised me, the path I had walked countless times, the doorway where my grandmother prayed, and the yard where my childhood lived.

Years later, I would find words that explained the kind of hope I needed that morning. Jeremiah 29:11 (NIV) says, "For I know the plans I have for you," declares the Lord, "plans to prosper you and not to harm you, plans to give you hope and a future." At the time, I did not know that verse, but I needed that promise. I needed to believe that leaving was not abandonment. I needed to trust that God could hold my future the way my family held my heart.

As we drove away, everything familiar disappeared through the window. First the road, then the house, then the figures of the people I loved, growing smaller until they were gone. It felt like my soul was tearing in half. I did not feel brave. I felt broken. But beneath the fear, there was a quiet whisper, the same whisper that had followed me since the dream, reminding me that I was not leaving alone. Later, I would read Hebrews 13:5 (NIV), where God says, "Never will I leave you; never will I forsake you." That was exactly what I needed, because the brokenness became the doorway to everything God would build afterward.

I did not know what was waiting for me in the next chapter. I did not know how deeply the transition would test me or how loneliness, language, and fear would try to steal my identity. I only knew what God had already proven to me. He stopped me in a dream and told me He was not done. And if He was not done, then this leaving was not the end. It was the beginning.

I was not ready for the impact leaving would have on me. I thought I was simply traveling to a new place, but I was stepping into a new identity. The road that carried me away from my home felt like a line being drawn between who I was and who I would have to become. I sat quietly, watching familiar trees and paths fade behind me, and felt a mix of grief and responsibility settle in my chest. I was leaving people who loved me deeply, but I was also carrying their prayers like luggage I could not put down.

Inside me, questions rose like waves. Would I ever return? Would my grandmother still be alive the next time I saw her? Would my aunt's laughter still fill the air when I came back? Would my father still be standing in that doorway with the same quiet strength? I did not speak those questions out loud because I did not want to make the pain heavier for anyone else. I carried them in silence, and I learned early that strength does not mean feeling nothing. It means feeling everything and continuing forward.

As the journey continued, I kept replaying my father's voice in my mind. "Everything will be alright." He had said it so many times when food was low, stress was heavy, and the future looked uncertain. Now those words had become a seed inside me. I did not fully understand faith, but I was learning it through him. Later, when I came to know Scripture, I would understand why his words carried such weight. "God is our refuge and strength, an ever-present help in trouble," Psalm 46:1 (NIV), and that is exactly how my father lived, even before he preached it. He moved like a man who believed help could come at any moment, even when trouble seemed permanent.

When the time came for the final goodbyes, it felt like my heart was being pulled in two directions. Part of me wanted to run back into my grandmother's arms and stay there forever. Another part of me felt the pull of destiny, as if God were nudging me forward, not with harshness, but with purpose. I did not know how to explain it. I only knew I could not stay the same, and I could not stay in the same place.

I remember turning around one last time, trying to lock the image into my mind. My grandmother stood with a face full of love and sorrow. My aunt wore a brave smile, but her eyes betrayed her true emotions, revealing pain she struggled to conceal. My father stood still, trying to be strong, not because he did not feel, but because he felt too much. In that moment, I understood something I could not have explained as a child. Love is not only about closeness. Love is also about sacrifice. Sometimes love releases what it wants to hold because it believes God's plan is bigger than its own fear.

Later, I would read that "faith is confidence in what we hope for and assurance about what we do not see," Hebrews 11:1 (NIV), and I would realize that even as a child, that was exactly what I was doing without having the words for it. I was stepping into something I could not see, carrying hope like a fragile candle, praying the wind would not blow it out.

The truth is that my childhood ended earlier than it should have. Life forced me to grow up quickly. Pain made me think deeper. Loss made me ask questions most children never ask, and responsibility pressed on me before I had the strength to carry it. Even in that, God was preparing me. I can see now that what felt like heaviness was also training. What felt like pressure was shaping. And what felt like a broken beginning was God laying a foundation.

Looking back, I believe God spoke to me that night because He knew what I would face later. He knew I would need an anchor when the storms arrived. He knew fear would try to convince me that my story was finished. He knew disappointment would try to tell me I was disqualified. He knew loss would try to make me bitter. Before any of that could happen, He gave me a message that would outlive every storm: "Go back. It is not your time. I am not done with you yet."

That sentence became the invisible rope that kept me from falling. It stayed with me in moments when food was scarce, grief was heavy, the future felt uncertain, and my mind imagined the worst. It reminded me that my life was not an accident. It reminded me that my survival was not luck. It reminded me that there was an assignment attached to my breath.

I did not understand calling back then, but I understand it now. God does not preserve people without purpose. When God saves you, it is not only to rescue you from what is behind you. It is also to prepare you for what lies ahead. I believe that is why He stopped me in that dream. He was not rejecting me. He was protecting me. He was telling me that my life belonged to Him, and because it belonged to Him, my story could not end early.

Even now, when I think about that season, I realize the island was not only the place where I was born. It was the place where faith began forming in me without my awareness. Faith was not a church service for me at first. Faith was my father's endurance. Faith was my grandmother's prayers. Faith was my aunt's encouragement. Faith was a boy whispering hope into the dark. Faith was God speaking one sentence that held me together.

It was there that I learned pain can be a teacher, but it does not have to be a prison. I learned that even when life is hard, God is still present, still speaking, still guiding, and still building something greater than what I can see.

When I stepped onto the path that led away from home, with fear in my chest and tears behind my eyes, one truth remained steady within me. If God was not done, then what came next would not destroy me. It would shape me. It would stretch me. It would prepare me for a life I could not yet imagine, but one He had already seen. I did not know the road ahead, but I knew the One walking it with me. That was enough to take the next step.

CHAPTER 2

FOUNDATIONS THAT SHAPED ME

I was raised between two worlds under the same sky. One world was shaped by discipline, responsibility, structure, and strength. The other was shaped by tenderness, warmth, laughter, and a kind of love that spoke without words. These two worlds existed side by side, separated only by a small yard and a narrow path I walked every day. On one side stood my father, a man whose life was defined by sacrifice and survival. On the other side lived my grandmother and my aunt, women whose presence softened the weight of life and gave me space to breathe.

Although my grandmother and aunt lived next door, their home felt like the center of my emotional world. I spent more time there than in my own house. My father often left before the sun rose and returned long after it had set, fighting every day to keep food on the table and a roof over our heads. His work was his language of love. His absence was not neglect. It was sacrifice. As a child, I could not understand that distinction. I only felt the quiet ache of missing someone who was always tired and carrying more than he could show.

In my grandmother's home, life felt different. The moment you stepped inside, comfort settled over you. The smell of food cooking filled the air, blending with laughter and gentle conversation. There was a calm that lived in that house, a peace that did not need explanation. They did not treat me as a responsibility. They treated me like a gift. They filled emotional spaces inside me that I did not yet know how to name.

My grandmother was the heart of everything. Her presence alone could quiet storms inside me that I did not yet understand. She spoke slowly, with wisdom shaped by years of endurance. When she prayed, it felt as though heaven leaned closer. When she looked at me, I felt seen. When she held my face between her hands, the world seemed to pause. Her love was firm but gentle, steady but warm. Looking back now, I understand why Scripture says, "The Lord is close to the brokenhearted and saves those who are crushed in spirit," Psalm 34:18 (NIV). Even when I did not know the words, I lived their truth through her.

My aunt was different in spirit but just as powerful in influence. She carried joy like a flame that refused to burn out. Her laughter filled rooms and chased away heaviness. She encouraged me constantly, pushing me to believe in myself even when life offered little evidence that belief made sense. She had a gift for turning difficult moments into laughter and silence into celebration. Around her, life felt lighter. Where my grandmother taught me steadiness, my aunt taught me joy.

Together, they formed the foundation of my emotional world. They gave me what my heart needed, while my father gave me what my future needed. I see now that God placed them around me intentionally. He knew I would need both strength and softness to survive what was coming. He knew I would need discipline to endure and tenderness to remain human.

Every morning before school, I walked the short path between our homes. Some mornings began before sunrise. I carried heavy buckets of water across uneven ground, the weight pulling against my arms while sleep still clung to my eyes. Carrying water was more than a chore. It was training.

Carrying those buckets taught me patience before it taught me strength. The path was uneven, and if I rushed, water would spill and the weight would shift against my arms. I learned quickly that speed created more pain, not less. Each step required balance, focus, and control. Some mornings my hands cramped and my shoulders burned, but stopping was not an option. There was no audience, no praise, and no reward waiting at the end.

The work itself was the lesson. I was learning that responsibility does not wait for comfort and that showing up consistently matters more than how you feel in the moment. It taught me responsibility before I understood the word. It taught me discipline before I knew its value. It taught me that strength is built through repetition and effort.

My grandmother would meet me and wipe the sweat from my forehead, telling me I was strong even when my arms were shaking. My aunt would press bread or fruit into my hands and tell me not to be late. Their voices were encouraging. They were shaping my confidence without speeches or lessons, simply by being there.

My father shaped me differently. His hands were rough from labor, his eyes carried worry he tried to hide, and he did not speak much. Affection was not something he expressed openly, but his love was evident in sacrifice. He worked so we could eat, and his silence was not rejection. It was responsibility. His distance was not an absence of love. It was the cost of survival.

During the rainy season, mornings often began with dread. Heavy rain turned the roads into rivers of mud, swallowing shoes and staining school uniforms. I would stand in the doorway, staring at the rising water, feeling defeated before the day even began. Without a word, my father would bend down and motion for me to climb onto his back. Rain soaked his clothes as he carried me through mud and water, step by steady step, until the ground was firm enough for me to walk alone.

What stayed with me was not just that he carried me, but how he carried me. His steps never hurried, even when the rain poured harder. He adjusted his footing with care, making sure I was steady before taking the next step. I remember the sound of water splashing beneath his feet and the quiet determination in his posture. In those moments, I felt safe without him ever saying a word. That kind of security shapes a child in ways words never can. It taught me that trust is built through action and that real protection often comes silently, without explanation or acknowledgment.

Those mornings became our language. He never complained, never paused, or asked for acknowledgment. He carried the weight so I could walk clean into opportunity. I did not understand it then, but now I see the truth of what Scripture says: "Love always protects, always trusts, always hopes, always perseveres," 1 Corinthians 13:7 (NIV). I lived that verse before I ever read it. God was teaching me that real love does not announce itself. It acts. It carries. It endures.

Through those repeated walks in the rain, God was shaping something deeper inside me. He was teaching me what leadership looks like. Leadership means carrying others through difficulty. Leadership means walking through discomfort so someone else can stand with dignity. Leadership means enduring quietly so another person can move forward with confidence.

As I look back now, I see that God was forming me long before I recognized His hand. Compassion was built through my grandmother and my aunt. Resilience was built through my father. Discipline was built through responsibility. Faith was built through example, not sermons.

Everything around me was preparation for a future that would demand every lesson I was learning without knowing it.

It was also shaped by absence. There were questions inside me with no clear answers, questions I did not yet know how to ask, but ones that quietly lived beneath the surface of my childhood. Even surrounded by love, discipline, and structure, there were spaces inside me that felt unfinished.

Although I lived in a home with my father and my younger sister, I was not truly an only child. My mother had four other children who lived far away, in places I had never seen. They were my siblings by blood, yet they existed more like ideas than people in my mind. I did not remember their faces. I did not remember their voices. I did not remember playing with them or being held by them. I knew they existed because I was told they did, but knowing and belonging are not the same thing.

As a child, I did not have the language to describe what that separation did to me. I only knew that something felt divided. Somewhere in the world were brothers and sisters who shared my blood but not my memories. They belonged to me, yet they were distant.

That distance created questions I carried quietly. I wondered what it would feel like to grow up alongside them, to share daily life rather than shared blood alone. I imagined conversations we never had and memories that never formed. At times, I felt full of family and empty at the same time. That contradiction lived inside me without resolution. It taught me early that relationships are not defined only by connection, but also by absence. It also forced me to learn how to hold love for people I could not reach without letting that distance harden my heart.

I often wondered what they looked like. I wondered if they laughed like me, if they walked like me, and if they carried the same quiet questions in their hearts. I wondered if they ever thought about me the way I sometimes thought about them.

There were moments when that awareness created confusion inside me. I belonged deeply to my father's house, to my grandmother's prayers, to my aunt's laughter, and to the routines that shaped my days. Yet at the same time, I felt connected to people I could not see or reach. Part of me felt rooted. Another part of me felt scattered. I was learning early that identity can be complex, especially when love is spread across distance.

Mornings began early. Responsibilities were not optional. Carrying water, helping with chores, and preparing for school were simply part of life. There was no discussion about whether I felt like doing these things. They were expected. Through that expectation, discipline quietly took root. Those routines were shaping something essential inside me. They taught me that life does not pause because you are tired. They taught me that effort matters, even when no one is watching. They taught me that responsibility is often the seed of purpose.

In my grandmother's home, discipline looked different. It was softer, but no less powerful. She corrected without crushing. She guided me without shaming. Her words were measured, and her presence was steady. When she prayed, it was not loud or dramatic. It was consistent. Her faith did not come from sermons. It came from trust built over time. She believed God in ordinary moments, and that belief became an anchor in our family.

I watched my grandmother speak to God as if He were near. I watched her trust Him with small things and large burdens alike. Without realizing it, I learned that faith is not only about what you say. It is about how you live when life is uncertain. Years later, I would understand the truth of Proverbs 3:5–6 (NIV), "Trust in the Lord with all your heart and lean not on your own understanding." Long before I could quote it, I was watching it modeled.

My aunt's influence continued to balance the seriousness that life required. She reminded me that joy was not irresponsible. It was necessary. She laughed even when circumstances did not invite laughter. She found light in moments others might overlook. Through her, I learned that surviving is not the same as living. She showed me that joy can coexist with hardship, and that laughter does not mean you are unaware of pain. It means you refuse to let pain define you.

My father remained the quiet pillar beneath everything. His consistency never wavered. Even when food was scarce, even when exhaustion lined his face, he showed up. He did not complain. He did not explain himself. He simply did what needed to be done. His life preached without words. And though I did not know it at the time, he was teaching me that leadership begins with sacrifice.

There were evenings when I watched him sit quietly, his body finally resting after a long day. He rarely spoke about his worries, but I could feel them. Children notice more than adults realize. I could sense the pressure he carried, the responsibility he bore, and the love that drove him forward even when life offered little in return. In those moments, something settled inside me. I wanted to become a man who carried responsibility the same way, without bitterness, without resentment, and without abandoning those who depended on him.

Through all of this, God was forming my understanding of strength. Strength was not loud. Strength was not aggressive. Strength was consistent. Strength showed up every day. Strength carried others when they could not carry themselves. And strength, I was learning, often grows quietly, hidden inside ordinary routines and repeated sacrifice.

I did not know then that life would soon stretch beyond everything familiar. I did not know that separation would test these foundations. I did not know that the lessons learned in quiet yards, muddy roads, and humble homes would one day be the very things that kept me standing. But God knew.

I also became more aware of myself. I noticed that I did not move through life the same way other children did. While others laughed freely and played without concern, I often found myself thinking deeply, questioning quietly, and observing carefully. I enjoyed playing, especially soccer, but even then, there was a seriousness beneath the joy. It was not sadness. It was awareness. It was the sense that life mattered and that time was not something to waste.

Soccer remained one of the few places where my mind felt completely free. Running barefoot across dusty fields with friends allowed me to release the weight I carried inside. The ball became a temporary escape from responsibility. For a short while, laughter drowned out questions. Yet even in those moments, I was learning lessons. I was learning teamwork, discipline, and perseverance. I was learning how to push through exhaustion, how to fall and get back up, and how to keep moving even when my body wanted to stop.

I also became more aware of how absence shapes a person. The distance from my mother and my other siblings remained a quiet presence in my life. I did not speak about it often, but it lived in the background of my thoughts. It shaped my understanding of loss, longing, and emotional restraint. I learned how to carry questions without answers and how to live with uncertainty without collapsing under its weight.

During those years, faith continued to form in subtle ways. It was not yet expressed through formal belief or doctrine. It was expressed through trust. I trusted my father's consistency. I trusted my grandmother's prayers. I trusted my aunt's encouragement. Without realizing it, I was learning to trust God through the people He placed around me.

In hindsight, I see how Scripture echoes my experiences and the lessons I learned. "Train up a child in the way he should go, and when he is old, he will not depart from it" Proverbs 22:6 (NIV). At the time, I did not know this verse, but I was being trained through life itself. Every responsibility, every correction, and every act of love was shaping the direction of my future.

I found myself paying closer attention to the world around me. I noticed the way seasons change. I noticed how people adapt. I noticed how life demands growth whether you are ready or not. These observations shaped my patience and resilience. I learned that change is rarely announced. It often arrives quietly, long before it becomes visible.

I loved the familiarity of my surroundings. I loved the people who raised me. Yet at the same time, I felt a subtle pull toward something beyond what I could see. I did not understand it, but I respected it. I learned not to resist what I could not yet define.

Through it all, the foundations that shaped me remained steady. Discipline anchored me. Love softened me. Responsibility strengthened me. Faith quietly took root. These elements worked together, forming a balance inside me that would soon be tested. God was not rushing the process. He was building it carefully, layer by layer.

I did not know then that these foundations would soon be stretched beyond their comfort. I would be required to stand on my own in ways I had never experienced. But God knew. He was preparing me, not by removing hardship, but by strengthening what He had already placed within me.

Nothing in my daily routine announced that change was coming. Everything around me looked the same, with the same responsibilities, the same familiar faces, and the same steady rhythm of life continuing as it always had. Yet deep inside me, something felt unsettled, not with fear or confusion, but with purpose. It was as if I was standing on solid ground while the path ahead was beginning to stretch into something greater than I understood at the time.

I did not talk about these feelings with anyone. I did not know how. I learned early that some things are carried internally before they are ever spoken out loud. Instead, I watched, listened, and reflected. I paid attention to moments that once felt ordinary, sensing they held more meaning than I had previously realized. It felt important to remember, to observe, and to absorb.

I noticed how my grandmother's prayers remained consistent, even when circumstances did not improve. She prayed with the same calm whether days were easy or difficult. Through her, I learned that faith does not fluctuate with outcomes. Faith remains steady even when results are delayed. Without knowing it, I was learning what it meant to trust God beyond immediate answers.

I watched my aunt continue to bring joy into spaces where joy did not seem logical. Her laughter did not deny reality. It challenged it. She refused to let hardship have the final word. Through her, I learned that hope is not passive. It is an active decision to believe that light still matters, even when darkness is present.

I observed my father with growing understanding. I began to recognize the weight he carried and the choices he made each day. His sacrifices were no longer invisible to me. I saw the cost of his endurance. I understood that his silence was not emotional distance, but discipline. He was teaching me that responsibility often requires restraint, and that strength sometimes means standing firm without explanation.

These realizations changed the way I viewed my life. What once felt routine began to feel intentional. What once felt like obligation began to feel like preparation. I sensed that every experience was shaping something not yet revealed. God was building me quietly, deliberately, and thoroughly.

As I consider this now, I see the wisdom in the words of Ecclesiastes 3:1 (NIV), "There is a time for everything, and a season for every activity under the heavens." Though I did not know this verse then, I was living its truth. My childhood had a purpose, a season that shaped me in ways I could not fully grasp at the time.

There were moments when I felt both grateful and restless. I was thankful for the stability I had, yet aware that life would eventually require more from me. I did not know what that "more" looked like. I only knew that I was prepared to respond when the time came. That awareness did not frighten me. It strengthened me.

I began to understand that foundations are not built for comfort. They are built for weight. Everything that had shaped me, discipline, love, responsibility, absence, faith, and endurance, was being placed into my life so I could stand when pressure arrived. God was not wasting time. He was not rushing me either. He was doing careful work that cannot be undone later, not with drama, but with maturity.

The boy shaped by protection was becoming someone aware of responsibility beyond his surroundings, someone learning that lessons formed in quiet spaces are meant to prepare you for louder challenges ahead. The foundations were firm, and what had been built inside me was strong enough to carry the weight of whatever came next.

I did not yet know where life would take me next. I did not know what would be required of me. But I knew this: what had been built inside me would not collapse when change came. The people who raised me had given me more than memories. They had given me stability, values, and a framework strong enough to hold my future.

CHAPTER 3

WHEN FEAR BECAME MY TEACHER

Fear did not arrive at once. It crept quietly, disguised as unfamiliarity, confusion, and the constant awareness of being out of place. Nothing from my childhood had prepared me for how disorienting it feels to be surrounded by people yet feel completely unseen. The world I stepped into moved faster, spoke louder, and expected confidence before understanding.

The first thing that struck me was the cold. It was not just the temperature, but the way it settled into my body, sharp and unwelcoming. Wind cut through my clothes, carrying sounds I did not recognize and energy I could not yet match. The air felt heavier than anything I had known, and with every breath, it became clear that survival here would require something different from what had sustained me before.

Everything moved quickly. Cars rushed past without pause. People walked with purpose, eyes forward, conversations clipped and efficient. There was no lingering, no casual acknowledgment, no shared familiarity. The streets felt crowded but distant at the same time. For the first time in my life, anonymity pressed against me. No one knew my name. No one knew my story. No one knew what I carried inside.

The apartment where we lived was small, crowded, and loud. Walls were thin, and sounds traveled easily. Sirens echoed constantly through the night, slicing through silence and sleep alike. Heat pipes clanged without warning. Voices from neighboring apartments bled through the walls, blending into a constant hum of movement. Rest did not come easily. Familiar quiet was gone, replaced by noise that never seemed to stop.

Nighttime became the hardest. Lying awake, listening to the city breathe, memories of home surfaced without permission. My grandmother's prayers echoed in my mind. My aunt's laughter replayed softly in my thoughts. My father's steady presence, once taken for granted, now felt distant and unreachable. The foundations that had shaped me were suddenly far away, and the separation felt deeper than distance alone.

Questions circled endlessly without answers. Did I belong here? Would I be able to adapt? Could the boy shaped by discipline, responsibility, and quiet strength survive in a place that demanded speed, confidence, and self-assertion? Nothing about this world felt familiar, and familiarity had always been my anchor.

Language became another barrier. The words sounded different, accents carried meanings I did not yet understand, and conversations moved so quickly that there was little room to ask questions without feeling exposed. Silence became safer than speaking incorrectly, and observation became protection. Just as in childhood, watching and listening took precedence over expression.

Fear began to teach lessons early. It taught me awareness. It taught me caution. It taught me humility. Confidence was no longer assumed; it had to be earned. The stability I once felt through routine and structure was replaced by constant adjustment, and every day required effort simply to keep up.

Despite the fear, something familiar remained alive inside me. The discipline built through responsibility did not disappear. The endurance shaped by hardship did not vanish. The faith planted through example, not words, still existed, even if it felt quieter. The foundations laid in childhood had not been removed. They were being tested.

School introduced another layer of pressure. New expectations collided with internal uncertainty. Classrooms felt overwhelming, filled with voices and systems I did not yet understand. Learning was no longer just about knowledge. It was about proving worth in an environment that did not stop asking where you came from.

Even surrounded by people, connections felt distant. Familiar faces were gone. Cultural cues were different, and what once felt natural now required conscious effort. The absence of grounding voices made fear louder, and without realizing it, fear began shaping my behavior.

Yet fear did not destroy me; it sharpened me. It forced attention inward and demanded growth. It exposed weaknesses that comfort had never revealed. Every unfamiliar moment pressed against the foundations built long before this season. The lessons from my father, my grandmother, and my aunt began to surface quietly, not as memories, but as survival tools. Strength was no longer theoretical. It was required.

The boy who had learned to carry responsibility was now learning to carry fear. Through that process, something deeper was forming. Fear was no longer just an emotion. It was becoming a teacher, revealing limits, demanding courage, and preparing me for battles I did not yet understand. This was no longer childhood. This was initiation.

The days that followed did not offer relief from fear. Instead, fear settled into my routine, becoming something I carried rather than something I reacted to. It followed me into classrooms, onto crowded streets, and into quiet moments when my thoughts had too much room to wander. Life demanded adjustment at a pace that felt relentless, with little space to slow down or reflect. Every environment required alertness, and every interaction felt like a test I had not studied for.

Expectations were unspoken but firm. Students moved with confidence, speaking freely and responding quickly, while I measured every word before allowing it to leave my mouth. Accents, expressions, and cultural references passed me by, leaving me feeling as though I was always one step behind. Silence became my shield. Observation became my strategy. It was easier to watch than to risk being misunderstood.

I noticed how people established belonging through confidence and how quickly weakness could be sensed. I learned that uncertainty is rarely met with patience. This world valued self-assurance, even when it was hollow, and I did not yet know how to perform confidence without betraying who I was. Instead, I leaned on what had been built inside me long before this season arrived. Discipline kept me focused. Responsibility kept me grounded. Endurance kept me moving forward when retreat felt tempting.

Loneliness grew quietly. It was not dramatic or overwhelming at first, but persistent and heavy. Even surrounded by people, connection felt distant. Familiar voices were gone, replaced by unfamiliar rhythms and expectations. The warmth I once felt from community was replaced by independence that felt premature. The absence of my grandmother's prayers, my aunt's encouragement, and my father's steady presence created a silence that echoed inside me.

In that silence, fear found space to speak. It questioned whether I belonged, whether I was capable, and whether the foundations that shaped me would be enough to sustain me here. Yet even as fear pressed in, something deeper resisted collapse. The lessons learned in childhood did not disappear under pressure. They adapted. Responsibility became resilience. Discipline became structure. Faith became quieter, but it did not leave.

Faith during this season did not look like certainty. It looked like endurance. It looked like continuing forward even when understanding was limited. It looked like remembering that survival itself was evidence that God had not abandoned me. Long before I understood Scripture, I had learned through life that stability does not come from environment alone. It comes from what is built inside you.

Removed from familiar surroundings, I was forced to confront who I was without reinforcement. There were no familiar roles to lean on and no community that automatically recognized my value. Identity could no longer be inherited from surroundings. It had to be formed internally. This realization was unsettling, but necessary. It exposed the difference between who I had been shaped to be and who I would have to choose to become.

In those moments, memories of home surfaced without warning. The image of my father walking through mud without complaint returned often, reminding me that endurance had already been modeled for me. The sound of my grandmother's prayers echoed quietly in my mind, reminding me that faith does not require immediate answers to remain valid. The joy my aunt carried, even in hardship, reminded me that fear does not have to erase hope.

It no longer functioned only as a threat. It became a mirror, reflecting areas that required growth. It revealed weaknesses that comfort had concealed and forced development that familiarity had delayed. Through fear, I learned adaptability. Through fear, I learned humility. Through fear, I learned that courage is not the absence of fear, but the willingness to move forward despite it.

Childhood habits were tested against adult expectations. Emotional resilience was no longer optional. The foundations built through discipline, love, responsibility, and faith were no longer theoretical. They became practical tools for survival. Every day required applying what had been planted years earlier.

Fear did not arrive to destroy me. It arrived to refine me. God did not remove fear from my path. He used it to shape strength, deepen awareness, and prepare me for challenges that comfort alone could never provide. The boy shaped by protection was being introduced to a world that demanded courage, adaptability, and internal stability.

Fear became a teacher because it exposed truth. It revealed the difference between security rooted in surroundings and strength rooted in character. Through its lessons, I began to understand that what had been built inside me was not fragile. It was forming exactly as it needed to, preparing me for what lay ahead.

Nothing slowed down for my understanding. Conversations continued at full speed. Rules were enforced without explanation. Social cues were assumed to be obvious. The pressure to adapt quickly created a tension that lived beneath the surface of every interaction.

Language became one of the greatest barriers to confidence. Words formed clearly in my mind, but by the time they reached my mouth, they often felt tangled and incomplete. Each attempt to speak required courage because misunderstanding carried consequences, not always spoken, but felt. Laughter, confusion, or impatience could follow even the simplest effort, and that reality trained me to be cautious. Silence became a form of protection, not because I lacked thoughts, but because expression felt risky.

That silence, however, came at a cost. Holding everything inside created emotional weight with nowhere to go. Questions about identity grew stronger in the absence of familiar affirmation. Without the voices that once reminded me who I was, doubt attempted to redefine me. It suggested that value was tied to fluency, confidence, and belonging, qualities that now felt distant. The absence of reassurance created internal conflict, where strength and uncertainty existed side by side.

The discipline learned in childhood surfaced naturally, guiding my routine even when motivation was low. Responsibility, once learned through chores and survival, became the framework that kept me functioning. Structure offered stability when emotions fluctuated. These traits were not learned in this environment, but they proved essential within it.

Moments of isolation often led to reflection. Without distractions, the mind revisits memories with clarity. My thoughts returned frequently to the life left behind, not only with longing, but with recognition. The foundation built through sacrifice, prayer, endurance, and love had not disappeared simply because the setting had changed. It had become an internal compass, guiding decisions when direction felt unclear.

Gradually, I became aware that discomfort was not evidence of failure, but an indication of transition. Growth was taking place in unseen ways, reshaping my perspective and strengthening my internal resolve. Challenges that once felt overwhelming began to reveal lessons beneath the surface. Adaptation required patience, humility, and perseverance, qualities that had been planted long before this season arrived.

Faith during this time did not show itself through clarity or confidence, but through persistence. It existed quietly, sustaining effort rather than eliminating struggle. Trust was no longer tied to understanding outcomes, but to believing that purpose remained intact even when circumstances felt unstable. That belief did not remove difficulty, but it prevented collapse.

Interactions with authority figures, peers, and unfamiliar systems reinforced the reality that this environment demanded self-definition. Identity could no longer be inherited or assumed. It required intentional development. Each experience, whether affirming or discouraging, contributed to resilience. Character was no longer theoretical. It was being tested through lived experience.

Slowly, internal strength began to outweigh external intimidation. The ability to endure without retreat strengthened confidence, not in perfection, but in persistence. Vulnerability remained present, but it no longer controlled my movement. Growth occurred not through ease, but through consistent effort despite discomfort.

Looking back, this stage marked a shift from survival rooted in protection to survival rooted in adaptability. Childhood lessons were no longer preparation alone. They had become active tools used daily. What once felt like overwhelming pressure was refining awareness, discipline, and endurance in ways comfort never could.

This season did not remove uncertainty, but it reshaped my response to it. Instead of resisting discomfort, I began learning from it. Instead of retreating inward, I observed carefully and adjusted intentionally. Instead of waiting for confidence to arrive, I acted responsibly despite its absence.

The transformation was gradual, but unmistakable. Strength was no longer defined by surroundings or reassurance. It formed internally, grounded in everything that had been planted long before this chapter began.

There comes a moment in life when experiences stop being lessons observed from a distance and begin carving themselves into identity. That moment arrived unexpectedly, without warning, and without mercy. What followed did not simply challenge me. It confronted everything I thought I understood about safety, authority, belonging, and my place in this new world.

The encounter with law enforcement did not feel like an isolated event. It felt like the culmination of everything that had been quietly building since my arrival in this unfamiliar environment. Language, culture, skin color, posture, silence, and misunderstanding collided at once, creating a situation where control was no longer mine. Power shifted instantly, and I became aware of how small a person can feel when explanations are not requested and assumptions are already made.

In that moment, the world narrowed. Sounds blurred together. Movement felt restricted. Awareness sharpened around every detail, every expression, every command. There was no space for clarification and no opportunity to explain intention or context. Everything moved quickly, yet time felt suspended, stretching the experience into something far heavier than the moment itself.

What unsettled me most was not the physical presence of authority, but the realization that identity could be rewritten without consent. I was no longer seen as a child learning to adapt or a young person carrying displacement quietly. I was reduced to a perception shaped by unfamiliarity and bias, judged without understanding and categorized without context.

The internal impact lingered long after the external situation ended. Trust was shaken. Innocence fractured. The sense of protection once associated with adults and institutions weakened. Questions surfaced without immediate answers. What does safety mean when it depends on how others perceive you? What does obedience mean when it does not guarantee fairness? What does belonging look like when acceptance feels conditional?

That experience introduced a new awareness of vulnerability, one that could not be unlearned. It forced an early confrontation with reality, revealing that survival in this environment required more than discipline and effort. It required awareness, restraint, and the ability to read situations quickly, even when clarity was absent.

Yet even in that disruption, something deeper remained intact. The foundation built through sacrifice, responsibility, and quiet endurance did not disappear. It steadied my response. It prevented collapse. It held me upright when confusion could have pulled me under. Strength did not appear as defiance or resistance, but as composure, restraint, and the refusal to let that moment redefine my worth.

Faith, though not loud or expressive, became essential in its quiet persistence. Not as a shield from hardship, but as an anchor against internal unraveling. Trust in God during this time did not answer questions or erase tension, but it preserved identity when external forces attempted to distort it.

That moment marked a shift. Life was no longer approached with an assumption of fairness. Awareness replaced innocence. Caution replaced ease. Observation became instinctive. Yet bitterness did not take root, because purpose had already been planted too deeply.

Instead of closing off, the experience sharpened discernment. Instead of retreating into resentment, it reinforced resolve. Instead of weakening belief, it refined it. The encounter revealed how quickly circumstances can strip away comfort, but also how firmly a foundation can hold when it has been laid correctly.

Looking back, that moment stands as a dividing line between who I had been and who I was becoming. It did not define me, but it shaped me. It did not destroy trust, but it forced faith to mature. It did not silence purpose, but it clarified the kind of strength required to carry it forward.

This was no longer adaptation. This was awareness. This was growth through confrontation. And although the experience left marks that would take time to fully understand, it did not take what mattered most. Identity remained intact. Faith remained active. Purpose remained untouched.

What had been planted in childhood proved strong enough to withstand pressure in unfamiliar territory. Even as uncertainty expanded, the truth remained steady. This journey was not accidental, and this chapter, though heavy, was not the end. It was shaping the endurance needed for what would come next.

After the moment passed and the external tension dissolved, the internal work quietly began. Nothing about it was immediate or obvious. There was no dramatic breakdown and no visible reaction that announced what had taken place inside me. Instead, the experience settled slowly, embedding itself into thought patterns, posture, awareness, and the way I learned to move through the world from that point forward.

Daily life resumed on the surface, yet something fundamental had shifted underneath. Interactions were no longer approached with ease alone, but with calculation. Spaces were scanned differently. Tone, timing, and expression became considerations rather than instincts, not because confidence was lost, but because reality had introduced a new layer of responsibility.

The most difficult part was not explaining what happened to others, but understanding what it meant for me. There was confusion that did not seek attention, questions that had no clear place to land, and an awareness that certain protections I once assumed were universal were, in fact, conditional. This realization did not arrive as bitterness, but as sobering clarity.

It became evident that adaptation was not only about learning language, culture, or environment. Adaptation now required emotional intelligence, restraint, and discernment beyond my years. Survival depended not only on effort, but on perception. Strength was no longer measured by endurance alone, but by the ability to remain composed while processing contradiction.

Yet something remarkable occurred alongside this awareness. Instead of shrinking, identity began to consolidate. The discipline formed through childhood hardship, the steadiness learned from consistent responsibility, and the faith quietly planted long before this moment worked together to stabilize my inner world. Though shaken, it did not fracture.

Faith during this season did not manifest through answers or clarity. It existed as trust without explanation, as endurance without understanding, as the steady belief that identity was not determined by a single moment or external judgment. Scripture would later give language to this truth, reminding me that "the Lord is my light and my salvation, whom shall I fear?" Psalm 27:1 (NIV), a declaration not of invincibility, but of grounding.

What emerged from this season was not withdrawal, but maturity. Emotional responses slowed. Reactions became measured. Observation sharpened. Rather than surrendering to confusion, the experience taught me how to pause, assess, and choose restraint over impulse. Growth did not announce itself, but it became visible through behavior, awareness, and quiet resolve.

Authority was no longer viewed through innocence alone, nor was it rejected. Instead, it was understood as complex, layered, and human. Trust was not abandoned, but recalibrated. Respect remained, now informed by discernment rather than assumption.

This period taught that strength is not proven by resistance, but by regulation. Not by confrontation, but by composure. Not by volume, but by clarity of purpose. The ability to remain anchored while navigating uncertainty became one of the most valuable lessons of that chapter.

Gradually, confidence began to return, not as recklessness, but as stability. The world no longer felt entirely unpredictable because internal grounding had strengthened. The realization took hold that while circumstances could shift without warning, identity rooted in purpose remained intact.

Looking back, this stage of the journey served as a refining fire rather than a breaking point. It removed illusions without stripping hope. It introduced caution without extinguishing ambition. It deepened faith without demanding explanation.

What was once a moment of disruption became a foundation for discernment. What could have led to withdrawal instead produced awareness. What might have silenced growth instead sharpened direction.

Although the weight of the experience continued to echo in later chapters, it no longer held power over identity. It became part of the story, not its definition.

The journey forward would demand even more endurance, clarity, and trust, but this chapter had already accomplished its work. It strengthened the inner framework required to carry what was coming next.

With time, what once felt overwhelming began to settle into understanding. Not understanding in the sense of having answers, but understanding in learning how to live with unanswered questions without allowing them to dominate identity. The environment did not change immediately, and circumstances did not suddenly become easier, but something within me stabilized as I learned to trust my own judgment again.

School became one of the primary places where this internal rebuilding occurred. Every classroom carried reminders that I was still an outsider, still learning how to navigate language, expectations, and unspoken rules. Yet rather than shrinking from those challenges, attention sharpened. Observation became a quiet strength. Listening replaced reacting. Patterns emerged, and with them came confidence rooted not in ease, but in awareness.

Belonging no longer felt like something to demand or rush toward. It became something to grow into gradually. Instead of forcing acceptance, effort shifted toward consistency, discipline, and self-respect. Confidence developed not through approval, but through reliability. Each completed task, each moment of restraint, and each decision to remain focused added another layer of stability.

There were still moments of uncertainty, but they no longer carried the same weight. What once disrupted internal balance now served as a reminder of how much had already been endured. Perspective expanded. Challenges were no longer measured against comfort, but against resilience already proven. That shift quietly changed everything.

Trust in God during this period deepened without becoming dramatic. Faith functioned less as an emotional refuge and more as a steady foundation beneath daily life. Scripture later gave language to this progression, affirming that "the steps of a good man are ordered by the Lord, and He delights in his way" Psalm 37:23 (NIV). At the time, those steps felt uncertain, but they were moving forward nonetheless.

Slowly, confidence returned, not as boldness that sought attention, but as calm assurance that no longer required validation. Identity was no longer reactive. It became rooted. Instead of being shaped by the opinions or actions of others, it began aligning with values formed long before this chapter began. Discipline, responsibility, faith, and endurance reasserted themselves, not as defenses, but as guiding principles.

This stage of the journey taught that growth does not always arrive through dramatic change. Often, it appears quietly through consistency. Through waking each day and choosing to engage rather than withdraw. Through learning to speak when necessary and remain silent when wisdom calls for restraint. Understanding that strength is not proven by how loudly one responds, but by how steadily one continues.

Over time, the world felt less hostile, not because it softened, but because internal grounding strengthened. The ability to move forward without constantly looking over one's shoulder returned. Awareness remained, but it no longer dominated. It simply informed.

Looking back, this part of the journey marked the transition from reaction to intention, from survival to direction, from adjustment to growth. What had been introduced through disruption matured into discernment, shaping the mindset required for what lay ahead. The foundation laid in childhood, reinforced through hardship, and tested through confrontation had proven resilient. It was held. It adapted. It strengthened.

As this chapter ended, one truth remained clear: the lessons learned here would not remain confined to this season. They would carry forward, influencing decisions, relationships, and purpose long into the future. This was not the end of struggle, but the beginning of confidence grounded in experience rather than assumption. It was the quiet emergence of direction, shaped not by comfort, but by endurance.

CHAPTER 4

LEARNING WHO I WAS BECOMING

The transition into this stage of life did not arrive with ceremony or clear markers. There was no moment that announced growth or signaled a significant shift. Instead, change unfolded quietly through daily experience, shaped by routine, responsibility, and the steady pressure of expectation. Life moved forward without pause, and adaptation became less about survival and more about learning to function with intention in an environment that demanded awareness at every level.

The world I was now living in required a different kind of attention. Cultural differences surfaced not through obvious conflict, but through subtle interactions, tone, posture, and unspoken rules that governed behavior. What once felt natural needed reconsideration. Communication carried new weight, silence carried new meaning, and assumptions could no longer go unexamined. Learning to move through these spaces required patience, observation, and a willingness to adjust without losing identity.

Home life reflected the same intensity. Space was limited, privacy was scarce, and responsibility was shared by necessity rather than choice. Everyone carried weight, and contribution was expected regardless of age or comfort. Structure was not enforced through conversation but through circumstance. There was little room for hesitation. Life demanded participation.

School became a proving ground for this evolving identity. Language differences, cultural gaps, and expectations created moments of isolation, but withdrawal was not an option. Instead, awareness sharpened. Listening became deliberate. Behavior became measured. Each day presented lessons that extended far beyond academics, teaching discipline, restraint, and the importance of understanding context before responding.

Pressure began shaping perspective. What once felt overwhelming slowly became instructive. Experience replaced assumption, and observation replaced reaction. Rather than resisting the discomfort of adaptation, there was an unspoken acceptance that growth often arrives through tension rather than ease.

Confidence did not develop through recognition or approval. It emerged through consistency: showing up, completing tasks, remaining composed under pressure. These habits formed quietly, without applause, but they provided stability in an environment that rarely slowed down. Identity began anchoring itself not in circumstance, but in values shaped long before this chapter began.

Faith during this period continued evolving in form. It was no longer limited to moments of desperation or survival. It became orientation rather than escape. Trust in God did not remove difficulty, but it reframed it. Challenges were no longer viewed as opposition, but as part of formation. Direction mattered more than speed, and endurance mattered more than visibility.

This stage of life became less about proving anything to others and more about understanding internal alignment. Integrity, discipline, and self-awareness took precedence over impulse or reaction. The focus shifted from trying to fit in to learning how to stand steadily without losing adaptability.

Becoming was no longer an abstract concept. It was happening daily, shaped by responsibility, restraint, and the slow refinement of character. The future remained unclear, but direction was beginning to form quietly beneath the surface.

This chapter marks the season where identity stopped reacting to environment and began responding with intention. It was not arrival. It was preparation. It was the slow realization that growth does not announce itself, but reveals itself over time through consistency, awareness, and endurance.

The internal shift that had begun quietly started to influence the way decisions were made. Reactions slowed, not because uncertainty had vanished, but because discernment had taken its place. Experience had taught that not every situation required a response, and not every challenge demanded confrontation. Learning when to speak and when to remain silent became an essential skill, developed through observation rather than instruction.

The environment continued to test identity in subtle ways. Expectations were often unspoken, and mistakes carried consequences that were not always explained. Rather than allowing frustration to take control, attention turned toward understanding patterns. Consistency revealed more than emotion ever could. Stability became more valuable than approval, and reliability began shaping reputation long before intention did.

Responsibility expanded naturally during this period. Tasks were not assigned with ceremony, they appeared through necessity and remained until they were completed. Accountability became part of daily life, reinforcing the understanding that contribution was not optional. Through repetition, discipline stopped feeling restrictive and began providing structure. Structure brought clarity, and clarity created confidence.

Faith remained present without demanding attention. It functioned quietly, shaping perspective rather than dictating outcome. Trust in God influenced how setbacks were interpreted, not as signals to retreat, but as moments requiring patience and adjustment. Scripture would later affirm this understanding, stating, "Let perseverance finish its work so that you may be mature and complete, not lacking anything" James 1:4 (NIV). At the time, perseverance was not named, but it was practiced.

Relationships during this season changed in quality rather than quantity. Awareness of boundaries increased. Trust became measured rather than assumed. Respect was earned through consistency rather than performance. These adjustments did not create distance, but they introduced discernment. Understanding that not every connection carried the same weight brought balance and prevented unnecessary conflict.

Identity continued to strengthen through restraint rather than assertion. Confidence no longer relied on external validation, but rested in the ability to remain steady regardless of outcome. Pressure, once a driving force, no longer dictated behavior; it became a catalyst for growth and refinement, allowing a more intentional and purposeful approach to life.

Growth does not always come from gaining something new. Sometimes it comes from refining what already exists. The values planted early, discipline, responsibility, faith, and endurance, were not replaced. They were clarified.

Becoming was no longer reactive. It was intentional. And as this chapter continued unfolding, it became clear that preparation was still in progress. What was being built internally would soon be required externally. The foundation was setting, not for comfort, but for responsibility that had not yet arrived.

This season marked a deeper internal transition, one that could not be seen from the outside but was steadily reshaping everything inside. Life no longer felt like something that was simply happening to me. It felt like something I was being trained to navigate. Each experience added weight to discernment, and discernment slowly replaced impulse. Decisions were no longer driven by urgency or emotion, but by reflection and awareness developed through lived experience.

The weight of responsibility continued to grow, not suddenly, but gradually, as trust was built through consistency. Reliability began opening doors that talent alone never could. Showing up, finishing what was started, and maintaining discipline even when motivation was absent created a reputation that spoke without words.

Over time, it became clear that faithfulness in small things was shaping capacity for larger ones. This understanding would later align with Scripture, which teaches, "Whoever can be trusted with very little can also be trusted with much" Luke 16:10 (NIV). Long before encountering that verse, its principle was already shaping daily life.

Observation became one of the most valuable tools during this period. Watching how people responded under pressure revealed far more than listening to what they said. Systems functioned based on consistency, not emotion. Authority responded to reliability, not noise. Respect was built quietly through patterns of behavior rather than moments of performance. These realizations began shaping how effort was invested and where energy was conserved.

At the same time, internal questions began shifting in focus. Attention was no longer centered solely on survival, but on direction. Life was no longer measured by whether obstacles could be endured, but by what those obstacles produced. Growth became evident not because circumstances were easier, but because reactions were changing. Situations that once felt overwhelming were now approached with steadiness. The internal response was no longer panic, but evaluation.

Faith continued operating beneath the surface, steady and present. It was not dramatic, nor was it loudly expressed. It functioned as an anchor rather than a spotlight. Trust in God was no longer based on outcomes, but on character. The belief that God was shaping something purposeful through process brought patience during uncertainty. Scripture would later affirm this truth: "The testing of your faith produces perseverance" James 1:3 (NIV). Perseverance was not theoretical, it was being lived out daily.

This period also revealed the importance of restraint. Not every challenge requires explanation. Not every misunderstanding requires correction. Silence, when chosen intentionally, became a form of strength. There was power in remaining composed while pressure attempted to provoke a reaction. That composure was not weakness. It was control.

Identity continued forming quietly, not through declaration, but through alignment. Values established earlier were no longer just inherited; they were owned. Integrity became a decision made repeatedly, even when shortcuts were available. Discipline became internal rather than enforced, and growth no longer depended on supervision. It became self-sustaining, allowing for a more organic and authentic progression.

Through all of this, it became increasingly clear that preparation was still underway. Life was not yet demanding the full weight of what was being built, but the construction was intentional. Foundations were settling. Character was being reinforced. Capacity was expanding slowly and deliberately.

This stage of life began revealing a quiet but undeniable shift in how the world was processed internally. Experiences no longer passed by without reflection. Everything carried meaning, weight, and consequence. Actions created outcomes, words shaped environments, and choices echoed longer than expected. Life began teaching through patterns rather than isolated moments, and awareness sharpened with each repetition. Growth was no longer accidental; it was happening because attention had changed.

There was a growing understanding that maturity is not announced. It reveals itself through consistency, restraint, and the ability to remain grounded when circumstances attempt to destabilize direction. The pressure to react quickly began losing influence, replaced by the discipline to pause and assess. Pausing did not mean hesitation, it meant wisdom was beginning to take root. Situations that once demanded immediate response were now approached with measured thought, and that shift alone altered outcomes significantly.

Relationships during this season also revealed deeper truths. Some connections strengthened through shared values and mutual respect, while others gradually faded as priorities shifted. Distance did not always arrive through conflict; sometimes it came through clarity. There was growing recognition that alignment mattered more than familiarity. Shared history could not substitute for shared direction. This understanding was not born from bitterness, but from discernment.

Authority and structure were no longer seen as obstacles, but as frameworks that revealed character. Systems exposed discipline, accountability, and reliability. Those who resisted structure often struggled to advance, while those who learned to function within it gained access to opportunity. Observing this reinforced an important truth: freedom without discipline leads to limitation, while discipline creates space for growth. Scripture would later affirm this reality: "God is not a God of disorder, but of peace" 1 Corinthians 14:33 (NIV). Order was not restriction. It was alignment.

Internally, values continued solidifying. Integrity was no longer situational, it became foundational. Doing what was right was no longer dependent on visibility or reward. Character was being shaped in private, where no affirmation followed obedience. That unseen consistency built confidence that did not rely on approval. Strength was no longer borrowed from external validation; it was forming internally through conviction.

Spiritual awareness also deepened during this period. Faith matured from belief into trust. Trust no longer required explanation or reassurance. It existed quietly, rooted in the understanding that God was actively involved even when outcomes were delayed. Patience grew, not because answers arrived quickly, but because confidence in God's process increased. Scripture later described this posture clearly: "Those who wait on the Lord renew their strength" Isaiah 40:31 (NIV). Renewal was not sudden; it was gradual, steady, and lasting.

There was also a noticeable change in how challenges were interpreted. Difficulty was no longer seen as evidence of failure, but as part of development. Pressure became instructional rather than threatening. Each challenge carried information, revealing areas that required refinement. Growth no longer came from avoiding discomfort, but from learning to move through it with stability.

This period marked the development of internal leadership. Leadership was no longer tied to position or recognition. It was expressed through responsibility, reliability, and influence without force. Leading by example became natural rather than deliberate. Others began responding not to words, but to consistency. Trust formed quietly, built on repeated evidence rather than promises.

The process of becoming was not dramatic. It did not arrive with announcements or milestones. It unfolded quietly through repetition, discipline, and reflection. Each day added another layer, another lesson, another adjustment. Progress was steady, not rushed. Depth was forming before expansion.

Daily routines reshaped how responsibility was understood. Time carried new weight. Expectations were rarely explained, and patience was limited. Mistakes mattered, not because they were unforgivable, but because they revealed gaps in awareness that could not remain unaddressed. Observation became a tool for survival. Listening closely, watching carefully, and learning patterns proved far more valuable than speaking prematurely. Lessons were embedded in every hallway, every interaction, and every moment where silence carried instruction.

An internal dialogue developed, shaped by reflection rather than impulse. Identity was no longer anchored solely in where life had begun, but in how each day was being navigated. Early values did not disappear, they were being tested. Compassion had to coexist with caution. Strength needed to remain present without becoming rigid. Integrity had to be preserved without drifting into naivety. Each situation raised a quiet question: how much adaptation was possible without losing what mattered most?

Moments of isolation still surfaced, but their meaning shifted. Solitude became a space for recalibration rather than escape. Memory functioned as both anchor and reminder. The foundation laid earlier remained active, shaping responses even when surroundings felt disconnected from anything familiar. Lessons learned through responsibility, sacrifice, and quiet endurance were not lost, they were being repurposed for a new environment.

Confidence began forming in a different way. It no longer depended on certainty or control, but on the ability to remain steady amid uncertainty. Understanding grew through experience rather than explanation. There was a growing awareness that preparation often looks like confusion while it is happening, and clarity usually arrives later, after pressure has already done its work.

This phase did not offer resolution, but it established direction. The internal structure being built would later become essential. Ordinary days carried extraordinary weight, reinforcing resilience, discipline, and self-awareness. Nothing was wasted. Every moment contributed to the formation of something stronger than survival alone.

This period also introduced a deeper awareness of boundaries, not as walls built from avoidance, but as structures necessary for stability and clarity. Energy had to be protected. Attention had to be directed with intention. Not every situation required emotional investment, and not every voice carried wisdom. Learning when to engage and when to step back became just as important as learning how to move forward. Discernment began shaping choices quietly, guiding decisions long before consequences appeared.

Exposure to different perspectives expanded understanding without demanding agreement. Listening became more valuable than asserting opinions. Observing how people navigated pressure revealed character far more clearly than moments of comfort ever could. Some remained consistent and responsible when structure was required, while others unraveled under the same weight. Those contrasts reinforced a powerful truth: circumstances do not create character, they reveal it. That realization shaped how trust was extended and how expectations were managed.

Perspective continued maturing through repetition rather than sudden revelation. Lessons repeated themselves until they were understood. Situations that once produced frustration now invited evaluation. Reactions softened as understanding expanded. A growing awareness emerged: the ability to look beyond immediate outcomes and consider long-term implications. That shift did not remove difficulty, but it changed how difficulty was carried.

During this season, faith no longer required constant reassurance or visible confirmation. Trust operated quietly beneath the surface, steady even when progress felt slow and outcomes were unclear. This way of living would later be expressed in Scripture: "For we live by faith, not by sight" (2 Corinthians 5:7, NIV). That truth was already shaping daily decisions long before it had words attached to it.

There was also a growing recognition that growth often requires separation. Certain environments no longer aligned with the direction forming internally. Distance did not always come through conflict. Sometimes it came through clarity. Interests shifted. Priorities changed. Conversations evolved. Letting go did not feel dramatic; it felt necessary. Space created room for alignment, and alignment brought peace.

This stage was not marked by arrival, recognition, or certainty. It was marked by steadiness. The ability to remain grounded while navigating uncertainty became one of its defining features. Identity continued forming through action rather than declaration. Values were reinforced through choice rather than words. Integrity remained intact because it was practiced consistently, not because it was convenient.

What was being built during this time could not yet be fully seen, but it was becoming solid enough to support what lay ahead. Each experience added weight to discernment, strength to discipline, and depth to understanding. The process remained quiet, intentional, and necessary. The foundation was settling, preparing for the next stage of growth, one that would demand even more than this season had required.

Jean Joseph

CHAPTER 5

WALKING WITH GOD IN CONFIDENCE

There comes a point in a believer's life when faith can no longer remain internal. Belief cannot stay theoretical forever. Trust must eventually take shape through movement. Waiting has its place, but faith is proven when we walk forward carrying uncertainty with us. Many people believe in God in their hearts but remain emotionally attached to places, habits, or seasons God is asking them to leave behind. That tension creates spiritual stagnation. Faith was never designed to stay comfortable. At some point, agreement must turn into obedience.

God rarely explains everything before He calls us to move. He gives directions before details and instructions before clarity. Often, the invitation to step forward comes long before the destination is revealed. This is where trust is tested. Faith does not begin when everything makes sense. Faith begins when clarity runs out. God separates admiration from belief in moments like these. Admiration observes His power from a distance. Faith responds by moving toward Him, even when the path feels incomplete.

Many people pray for doors to open yet hesitate when those doors begin to move. The unknown feels threatening because it removes control.

Remaining still feels safer than stepping into unfamiliar territory, but safety is not the same as purpose. Nothing grows where growth has already ended.

God does not guide us into paths that guarantee ease. He leads us into paths that require dependence on Him. When we wait for ideal conditions, we delay what God is ready to do. When we demand the full plan before moving, we place our need for control above our trust in Him.

Every step taken in obedience releases strength that was not available before movement. What feels impossible while standing still becomes manageable once motion begins. God meets us in motion. He multiplies what we are willing to start. He breathes in effort, not intention. Breakthrough does not occur in hesitation. It unfolds in obedience.

Some voices come from within, shaped by insecurity and past failure. Other voices come from outside, shaped by fear and opinion. Doubt questions readiness. Insecurity highlights weakness. The enemy magnifies what we lack to freeze progress. But God's calling has never been based on human qualification. He does not choose people because they are ready. He chooses them because He is faithful. What God places inside a person is not dependent on their perfection but on His power working through their willingness.

He calls while we are still learning. He leads while we are still growing. He strengthens while we are still fighting. Willingness matters more than readiness. Obedience matters more than confidence. God develops capability along the way. Faith is not about arriving prepared. It is about trusting God enough to move.

Movement requires courage, and courage is not the absence of struggle. Courage is the decision to walk forward while uncertainty is still present. It is choosing truth over emotion and promise over fear. Courage does not wait for evidence. It walks toward what God has spoken. Every significant story of faith in Scripture begins the same way, with a step taken before understanding arrives. God responds to obedience. He honors motion. He reveals Himself along the path.

The steps matter more than intention. Plans and dreams hold no weight without action. God establishes what we are willing to move toward. Psalm 37:23 (NIV) says, "The Lord makes firm the steps of the one who delights in Him." Stability comes after movement, not before it. God strengthens the ground beneath those who step forward trusting Him. What once felt like risk becomes testimony. What once created hesitation becomes confirmation. God was never waiting to see if we were capable. He was waiting to see if we would trust Him enough to move.

A shift begins inside when belief moves away from anxiety and toward expectation. Anxiety focuses on what could fail. Expectation focuses on what God can do. Anxiety magnifies obstacles. Expectation magnifies God's ability. When anxiety leads, movement becomes cautious and restrained. When expectation leads, obedience becomes bold and intentional. Expectation does not require full understanding. It requires trust. It says God will do what He promised, even if the process is unclear.

Not forced confidence, quiet confidence rooted in trust. Confidence grows as faith is practiced, not announced. Each step taken builds internal strength. Each act of obedience reinforces trust. Faith becomes something lived, not discussed. And with each step forward, God reveals that He was already present in the places we were afraid to enter.

When faith begins to move, resistance often rises at the same time. The decision to walk forward exposes internal conflict that had been quiet while we remained still. Thoughts become louder. Old insecurities resurface. Memories of past failure attempt to regain authority. It is not because something is wrong, but because movement threatens what fear once controlled. Stillness allows fear to coexist peacefully. Obedience challenges it. The moment faith turns into action, the heart is forced to confront what it truly trusts.

Many people mistake this internal tension for a sign that they are doing something wrong. In reality, it often confirms that growth has begun. Faith exposes what comfort concealed. It reveals dependence we did not realize had formed and attachments we had justified as stability. God does not expose these things to shame us. He reveals them so they can be released. Growth always requires separation, not only from places and people, but from thought patterns that no longer align with where God is leading.

Anxiety is not always fear of failure. Sometimes it is fear of surrender. Faith demands the release of control, and control feels safe when life has been unpredictable. Many people learned survival through self-reliance, so trust feels risky. But God does not ask us to move forward while carrying everything alone. He invites us to release what overwhelms us so obedience does not become unbearable. Philippians 4:6 (NIV) says, "Do not be anxious about anything, but in every situation, by prayer and petition, with thanksgiving, present your requests to God." Anxiety loses authority when it is brought into God's presence instead of being carried in silence.

The focus begins to shift away from what could go wrong and toward what God has already proven. Reflection replaces reaction. Prayer replaces panic. Confidence grows quietly as trust deepens. This confidence does not come from personality or boldness. It is formed through repetition and obedience practiced daily in small, unseen ways. Faith becomes less about emotion and more about decision. The heart learns that God remains faithful regardless of circumstance.

Walking with God requires learning how to move without full visibility. Direction is often revealed one step at a time. God does not illuminate the entire path because faith would become unnecessary. Trust is developed through dependence, not explanation. Many moments require choosing obedience without understanding outcomes. That choice strengthens spiritual endurance. It trains the heart to rely on God's presence rather than predictable results.

Uncertainty does not mean God is absent. It often means He is developing trust. Faith grows strongest when answers are delayed. During those seasons, God is not withholding direction. He is shaping discernment. Learning to trust God's voice over visible evidence changes how decisions are made. Movement becomes intentional rather than reactive. Confidence settles into the soul, not because fear disappears, but because trust increases.

The internal battle between control and surrender continues until one becomes dominant. Control demands guarantees. Surrender requires trust. Control focuses on risk. Surrender focuses on obedience. God does not force surrender. He invites it. And when surrender is chosen, peace begins to replace strain. Trust removes the pressure to manage outcomes. Faith becomes lighter because it is no longer carried alone.

As obedience continues, perspective shifts. Challenges that once felt overwhelming begin to feel manageable, not because they shrink, but because trust grows. Strength increases internally before circumstances change externally. Faith builds resilience that cannot be shaken by temporary instability. Confidence develops through consistency. Each step reinforces the understanding that God is present in motion.

This growing trust reshapes identity. Belief moves beyond hope and becomes conviction. Faith is no longer something spoken; it becomes something lived. The heart learns that God is dependable even when outcomes remain unknown. Movement becomes less forced and more natural. Obedience becomes less intimidating and more instinctive.

This is the foundation of confidence, not self-assurance, but God-assurance. Confidence rooted in relationship rather than performance. Trust grounded in experience rather than emotion. As walking continues, faith becomes steady, not rushed. The soul settles into a rhythm of obedience that does not require constant reassurance. Each step taken reinforces the truth that God does not abandon those who trust Him. He walks with them. He strengthens them. He shapes them along the way.

Walking forward with God reshapes how pressure is handled. Pressure no longer feels like a signal to retreat but becomes a reminder to lean deeper into trust. Life does not suddenly become easier as faith grows, but it becomes more manageable because reliance shifts. Strength is no longer drawn from control or certainty but from the assurance that God is actively involved in every step taken. Confidence develops when trust becomes the default response instead of anxiety.

Moments arise when responsibility increases and expectations grow heavier. These seasons test whether faith is rooted in convenience or conviction. Trusting God when outcomes are unclear requires surrender of control. Surrender does not mean weakness. It means releasing the need to manage every detail and allowing God to lead beyond personal understanding. This kind of trust matures the believer and stabilizes the heart.

Confidence also brings clarity to relationships. Approval from others loses power. Validation is no longer required to continue moving forward. Walking with God teaches that obedience may not always be understood or supported by people. Faith matures when obedience continues without external affirmation. Trust becomes anchored in God's direction rather than human agreement.

Choices are no longer rushed out of fear or pressure. Discernment guides action. Prayer becomes instinctive rather than optional. Confidence removes the urgency to force outcomes and replaces it with steady obedience. Trust allows movement without panic and progress without striving.

Challenges still appear, but they no longer define direction. Setbacks no longer signal failure; they become moments of adjustment rather than discouragement. God often uses resistance to redirect rather than destroy. Confidence allows flexibility without loss of faith. Movement continues even when the path shifts unexpectedly.

This stage reveals that spiritual confidence is not loud or dramatic. It is calm, steady, and grounded. It does not need to announce itself. It is visible through consistency rather than performance. Confidence rests in knowing that God is present in the process, not only at the destination.

Walking with God brings freedom from pressure. Obedience replaces performance. Faith replaces comparison. Confidence becomes quiet assurance rather than loud self-promotion. There is peace in knowing that purpose does not require proving oneself to anyone.

Confidence does not come from what can be measured or predicted. It comes from trusting God beyond what is visible. Sight demands proof before movement, but faith moves while trusting God to provide clarity along the way. Living by faith releases peace because outcomes no longer determine direction.

Walking with God also sharpens discernment. Not every opportunity is meant to be pursued. Confidence allows discernment without guilt. Saying no becomes easier when purpose is clear. Faith matures when choices are guided by alignment rather than urgency. Discernment protects peace and preserves strength. Confidence grows when decisions are made prayerfully instead of emotionally.

Pressure still exists, but it no longer controls behavior. Confidence creates space to pause, reflect, and respond wisely. Emotional reactions give way to thoughtful responses. God's presence becomes the anchor during uncertainty. Stability replaces impulsiveness. Trust produces clarity even in complex situations. Confidence with God also brings endurance.

Seasons arise when progress feels slow and effort feels unnoticed.

Faith teaches perseverance without resentment. Strength is no longer dependent on motivation but on commitment. God uses endurance to deepen character. Confidence remains steady because it is built on trust rather than feelings.

This stage reveals that faith is not about arrival. It is about consistency. It is about walking forward without needing to see the entire path. God does His deepest work while trust is exercised daily. Confidence becomes the ability to remain faithful regardless of pace or visibility.

Walking with God in this way produces resilience. Setbacks no longer destroy momentum. Disappointment no longer defines direction. Trust continues even when circumstances shift unexpectedly. Confidence remains because God's faithfulness has already been proven.

Emotions are no longer ignored, but they are no longer allowed to rule. Fear, disappointment, and uncertainty are acknowledged without being given authority. Faith teaches that emotions can be felt without being obeyed. Stability develops when truth leads and feelings follow. Trust provides balance even when emotions fluctuate.

Decisions are no longer rushed or reactive. Movement is guided by alignment rather than urgency. Peace becomes confirmation instead of pressure. Discernment sharpens, allowing progress without haste and patience without stagnation. As distractions lose influence, God's direction becomes clearer.

Waiting begins to look different as well. Delays are no longer viewed as failure. Silence is no longer mistaken for abandonment. Faith recognizes that preparation often matters more than speed. Strength built slowly lasts longer than strength built quickly. Timing is understood not as restriction, but as protection.

Identity continues to settle into something stable. Approval is no longer chased. Worth is no longer measured by outcomes. Security grows from knowing who God is and who we are in Him, not from constant validation. This steadiness allows consistency even when circumstances shift.

Faith at this stage is not loud or dramatic. It is steady and grounded. It does not demand attention or constant reassurance. It holds firm without needing to prove itself. Trust produces endurance. Endurance produces wisdom. Wisdom produces peace.

Trust begins to shape daily discipline in subtle ways. Choices are no longer driven by urgency or pressure but by alignment. What once demanded immediate reaction now invites reflection. Silence becomes useful instead of uncomfortable. Stillness becomes strength rather than avoidance. Faith expresses itself not through grand declarations, but through consistent obedience in ordinary life.

Not every opportunity deserves a response. Not every voice deserves attention. Discernment grows as priorities become clearer. Energy is guarded. Focus sharpens. Life begins to feel less scattered because direction is no longer determined by emotion or impulse but by purpose.

There is also a deeper awareness of responsibility. Trust does not remove accountability; it strengthens it. Obedience requires consistency, especially when motivation fades. Discipline becomes an act of faith rather than willpower. Even when enthusiasm is low, commitment remains. Growth continues because faith is no longer dependent on feeling inspired.

Difficulty is no longer seen as opposition alone, but as refinement. Resistance is not always a sign to stop. Sometimes it is confirmation that movement is necessary. Pressure does not automatically signal failure; often, it signals development.

Prayer changes during this season. Requests become more honest. Language becomes simpler. The need to impress disappears. Conversations with God feel less formal and more real. Trust grows as communication deepens. Faith becomes relational instead of transactional.

There is also a noticeable shift in patience. Outcomes are no longer rushed. Waiting is no longer wasted. The process is respected because growth is recognized as essential. Progress may feel slow, but it is steady. Stability replaces anxiety. Direction replaces confusion.

Relationships begin to change as well. The need to explain everything fades. Silence no longer feels threatening. Not every struggle needs to be shared, and not every opinion needs to be addressed. Boundaries become clearer without being rigid. Peace becomes a guide for connection rather than obligation.

Decisions start to reflect patience instead of impulse. Time is taken before responding. Listening becomes more important than reacting. Wisdom grows quietly through experience rather than instruction. Direction becomes clearer because distractions lose their pull.

Trust also alters how effort is viewed. Work is no longer driven by fear of falling behind or proving worth. Effort becomes purposeful rather than exhausting. There is freedom to do what is required without carrying unnecessary pressure. This balance allows progress without burnout.

Life continues to unfold in ways that test trust in subtle forms. Some challenges are not dramatic or overwhelming. They are quiet and persistent, delays that stretch patience, decisions that require restraint, situations that offer no immediate resolution. These moments reveal whether trust has become internal or remains conditional.

There is a growing awareness that not every season demands action. Some moments require restraint rather than response. Silence becomes a choice instead of a reaction. Stillness no longer feels like avoidance, but alignment. Strength shows itself through restraint, not urgency.

The need to control outcomes weakens. Plans are held loosely. Expectations soften. Effort remains consistent, but attachment to results fades. Work is done faithfully without demanding immediate reward.

Peace becomes less dependent on progress and more rooted in presence. Directions are chosen carefully. Success is measured by alignment rather than appearance. Satisfaction comes from obedience, not recognition.

There is greater awareness of internal language. Thoughts are examined before being accepted. Negative assumptions lose authority. Hope becomes deliberate. Perspective widens enough to see that uncertainty does not equal danger. Unknown outcomes no longer provoke fear but invite patience.

Movement continues, not because everything is clear, but because reliance has become steady. Each step is taken with intention. The path may remain partially unseen, but direction no longer feels unstable.

Time reveals what pressure cannot. As days move forward, trust settles deeper into daily life. What once required effort now feels natural. Decisions are no longer filtered through anxiety or urgency, but through discernment shaped by experience. The pace of life steadies, not because challenges disappear, but because reactions change.

There is a growing comfort with not having immediate answers. Questions no longer create panic. Uncertainty no longer demands resolution. Waiting becomes productive rather than passive. Attention shifts from outcomes to faithfulness in the present moment. What matters most is staying aligned, not arriving quickly.

Relationships are handled differently in this stage. Conversations become more thoughtful. Boundaries become clearer without needing explanation. There is less need to be understood by everyone and more confidence in being led quietly. Approval loses its grip. Integrity gains weight.

Work continues with consistency, even when recognition is absent. Effort is offered fully, without resentment or expectation. Motivation is no longer driven by external validation but by inner clarity. Purpose feels stable, even when results fluctuate.

There is also a deeper awareness of rest. Rest is no longer avoidance or escape; it becomes intentional renewal. Stillness sharpens discernment. Reflection strengthens resolve. Space is created to listen rather than rush. Challenges still appear, but they no longer disrupt direction. Detours are met with flexibility. Adjustments are made without frustration. Progress is measured by growth, not speed. Stability replaces urgency.

Trust now lives beneath the surface. It informs choices without needing constant reinforcement. Faith no longer rises and falls with circumstances; it remains present, steady, and grounded.

What took shape in this chapter was not an ending, but a shift. The movement forward had begun, not because everything was clear, but because trust no longer depended on clarity. Walking with God was no longer something imagined or debated; it had become lived, practiced, and carried into ordinary days.

This season was not about reaching a destination. It was about learning how to remain steady while moving. Trust was no longer activated only in moments of pressure; it became part of daily decision-making, shaping how challenges were approached and how uncertainty was held.

The path ahead remained open. Questions still existed. Outcomes were not yet defined. But something important had changed internally. Dependence on control loosened. Attachment to immediate results softened. Forward motion continued without needing constant reassurance.

What followed next would require deeper discernment and greater endurance. The steps would not always feel light, and the road would not always feel familiar. But the foundation formed here made continued movement possible.

CHAPTER 6

THE YEARS THAT SHAPED ME

Vocational school gave directions, but it did not answer the bigger questions. A job came next, not because it felt like destiny, but because it was available, and stability felt urgent. The goal was simple: get on my feet, stop feeling behind, and prove that the people who doubted me were wrong. That is how the group home became my first real step into adulthood. The work was demanding, the hours were heavy, and the responsibility never waited for me to feel ready. The plan was always to stay for a little while. A little while became fifteen years.

The group home taught discipline the hard way. People depended on me every day, and their needs did not pause because I was tired, stressed, or uncertain. Patience had to become normal. Compassion had to become consistent. When situations became chaotic, calm had to show up, whether it was felt or not. That environment trained the mind to think quickly and the heart to carry weight. Leadership formed there, not in a classroom or a title, but in moments when everything could fall apart and someone had to remain steady.

From the outside, life looked fine. Work ethic earned respect.

Reliability became my reputation. People trusted me because I showed up, handled problems, and stayed composed. The problem was that the more dependable I became for everyone else, the more invisible I felt to myself. After long shifts, the house would be quiet, and the quiet would talk back. Nights ended with the same question that never truly went away: Is this really all my life is going to be?

Then the health problems began pushing their way to the surface. At first, it was easier to explain them away. Tiredness felt like stress. Shortness of breath felt like exhaustion from working too much. Tightness in my chest felt like something temporary. Keeping busy made denial easier. Working made it possible to ignore what the body was trying to say. But symptoms do not disappear because a person refuses to listen. They get louder.

So, life became something I tried to build with my own hands. Strength became the plan. Independence became the defense. Anything that resembled old spiritual pain was avoided. Yet even with all that distance, something kept stirring beneath the surface. At the time, it did not feel like God. It just felt like unrest that would not let me settle. Looking back, it was Christ speaking softly through the noise of routine, waiting patiently in the places I thought were empty.

The longer the years stretched, the heavier the pressure became. Knowing change was needed did not make change easy. Starting over felt risky. Failing felt embarrassing. Stepping into uncertainty felt like stepping into exposure. Still, there comes a point when staying becomes more painful than leaving. The pain of remaining the same started outweighing the fear of doing something new. Pretending became exhausting. The sense of being stuck became suffocating. Something had to break because it felt like I was the one breaking.

A decision formed, not with perfect confidence, but with desperation.

Dying with questions felt worse than failing with effort. The thought of spending an entire life wondering what could have been became unbearable. A quiet determination rose up that did not feel like pride; it felt like survival. Try. Move. Do something. That moment was not loud, but it was real.

College became the next step, even though it did not feel safe. Money was not saved. Academic confidence was not strong. Health problems made everything uncertain. Still, the application was filled out with trembling hands, and it was submitted anyway. That was faith before I had language for it, not the kind of faith that makes a person feel powerful, but the kind that simply refuses to remain stuck.

Stepping back into education after fifteen years away felt like standing at the edge of a cliff without a net. The mind tried to list every reason it would not work: too late. Too old. Too far behind. Too tired. Too broken. Yet something steadily kept whispering that being behind did not mean being finished.

Those years in the group home became defining, not because they were exciting, but because they forced a confrontation with what had been avoided. They revealed the gap between responsibility and calling. They exposed what routine can do to the spirit when purpose is ignored. They also showed me something else: even when life feels stalled, God can still be shaping what a person will need later.

My heart issues had been serious long before college became possible. In my twenties, my body felt older than my age. Pain in my chest could wrap itself around me like a fist. Some nights were spent listening to a heartbeat that felt unstable, wondering what would happen if it stopped while I slept. Doctor visits brought words like risk and limitation. Medication became part of life. Warnings came about stress and exhaustion, but responsibilities did not disappear just because my health was fragile.

Bills still needed to be paid. Work still demanded energy. People still depended on me. My mother still labored six days a week. Slowing down did not feel like an option. So I kept working. I kept showing up. I kept smiling. I learned how to function while broken.

That kind of survival creates a strange skill. It teaches a person to laugh while afraid, to keep moving while hurting, and to collapse only after everyone else is asleep. It also hardens the heart if it goes on too long. Suffering in silence does not heal anything. It only trains the mind to hide.

During that season, I was with the woman who would later become my wife. She walked beside me through years that were heavier than I admitted. She saw what others could not see. Still, even with her, pieces of pain remained hidden. Emotional armor had been built for so long that vulnerability felt dangerous. The fear was of breaking. The fear was that once broken, the pieces would never come back together.

Even with all that distance from faith, Christ was still present. That truth is easier to see looking back than while living through it. I did not feel Him the way I thought faith was supposed to feel. I did not pray the way I thought prayer was supposed to sound. Yet grace kept moving beneath the surface, softening what survival hardened and preparing what pain tried to destroy. It was the kind of grace that holds a person together when they do not even realize they are being held. Psalm 73:26 (NIV), "My flesh and my heart may fail, but God is the strength of my heart and my portion forever."

A shift began when the pain of staying the same became unbearable. Survival alone stopped feeling like enough. Something inside whispered that there had to be more than endurance. Direction was not yet clear, but the truth was. Remaining in the same place was no longer possible.

When 2016 arrived, my body stopped allowing denial. Pain became more constant. Breathing grew harder. Nights felt longer than days. Doctor visits multiplied, and the quiet fear I once hid began to surface. This was no longer discomfort that could be managed privately. This was the kind of struggle that demanded attention. It brought a question that hovered over everything: what if this is the end?

Hospital rooms, tests, medical language, and waiting rooms became part of daily life. Sitting in sterile spaces while doctors explained risk forces a person to face fragility earlier than expected. It brings questions most people try to avoid. Have I done enough? Did I waste time? What would my life mean if it ended now? The mind starts measuring everything differently when the body feels unstable.

Even then, faith did not look polished. There were no perfect prayers. Sometimes all I could say was a simple, desperate request for help. Sometimes there were no words at all. My body just breathed through the pain and let tears speak. Yet something sacred began waking up in the middle of that breaking. Christ was not watching from a distance. His presence was near, steady, and quiet, even when emotions were loud.

Psalm 94:19 (NIV): "When anxiety was great within me, your consolation brought me joy."

The day of surgery felt like stepping into another world. Cold rooms. Bright lights. A silence that grows heavy when the door closes. Thoughts of family, unfinished dreams, and time that cannot be reclaimed. Then the moment of letting go, the moment when control runs out and surrender becomes the only option.

When my eyes opened after surgery, the room felt both familiar and completely new. Machines, muted footsteps, the weight in my chest, the dryness in my throat, the strange feeling of being alive after facing what could have ended everything. Relief and confusion arrived together. Gratitude and fear arrived together. Tears came without warning, not only from pain, but from the reality that surviving changes a person in ways words cannot easily explain.

A decision formed in that hospital bed. Returning to my old life no longer felt possible. Going back to fifteen years of routine without fulfillment felt like returning to something slowly killing the spirit. Breathing is not the same as living. Surviving is not the same as becoming. A second chance could not be wasted on the same patterns.

Walking out of the hospital did not feel like returning to normal life. It felt like stepping into a version of the world that demanded honesty. Every movement required attention. Every breath felt deliberate. Strength was no longer something to assume; it had to be acknowledged as borrowed. The body moved slower, but awareness moved faster. Nothing felt casual anymore. Life no longer felt endless, it felt entrusted.

Leaving that job was not reckless. It was necessary. Security had already proven fragile. Health had already proven temporary. Continuing a life that no longer fit would have been a different kind of risk. Walking away meant choosing uncertainty over slow suffocation. It meant trusting that survival had not been granted just to return to the same limitations.

That season did not come with a clear blueprint. Direction arrived one step at a time. Boxes were packed. Familiar streets were left behind. Maryland became part of the past, and North Carolina became the unknown ahead. The move was not driven by comfort or preparation. It was driven by the understanding that staying still was no longer an option. Sometimes God does not remove fear before movement. Sometimes movement is what loosens fear's grip.

Buying a home in the middle of recovery did not feel logical. Opening a store in 2017 did not feel safe. Both decisions felt heavy with responsibility and light on certainty. Yet something steady held underneath the uncertainty. There was a sense that life was being rebuilt intentionally, even if the structure was not yet visible. Standing inside that empty space, surrounded by shelves and unfinished plans, carried the feeling that something new was being formed, not quickly, but honestly.

Education returned quietly. The desire to learn did not come from embarrassment or competition. It came from gratitude. Going back to school felt different this time. Learning was no longer about proving intelligence. It was about honoring the life that had been preserved. Classes became possible because they were online. Physical limitations made in-person attendance unrealistic. Even then, returning required courage. The mind still whispered doubts about age, gaps, and readiness. Yet those whispers no longer held authority.

North Carolina became a place of rebuilding. The pace slowed enough to allow reflection. Mornings carried a sense of intention rather than urgency. Recovery demanded patience, and patience began reshaping priorities. Life felt fragile, but it also felt purposeful. Faith started to move from background belief into lived dependence. The realization settled that survival had never been accidental. "When you pass through the waters, I will be with you, and when you pass through the rivers, they will not sweep over you." (Isaiah 43:2)

College became part of that rebuilding. Assignments, deadlines, and late nights returned, but the motivation had changed. Learning was no longer about escape. It was about alignment. Every subject felt connected to something deeper than grades. Knowledge began pointing toward purpose. The journey felt slow, but it felt right.

Then life shifted again in 2022. A run that began like any other ended without warning. Dizziness struck suddenly. Balance disappeared. The world tilted, twisted, and collapsed inward. The ground no longer felt stable. Consciousness faded. Waking up afterward brought confusion and fear that words struggled to contain. Vertigo entered life without introduction and refused to leave quietly.

Everything changed again. Movement became unreliable. Standing, walking, turning, and even opening my eyes on certain days became battles. Independence disappeared quickly. School paused. Work paused. Life slowed to a pace that felt unfamiliar and frustrating. The body could no longer be trusted to cooperate. Strength alone could not push through this kind of limitation.

Vertigo forced a different kind of surrender. Productivity had been part of identity for years. Now, stillness was unavoidable. The noise of busyness was removed. Silence returned, heavier than before. Questions surfaced that had been avoided for years. Identity could no longer be tied to output or endurance. Ability had proven temporary again.

Migraines joined the struggle, bringing pressure, light sensitivity, and moments when functioning felt impossible. Days varied. Some felt manageable. Others felt overwhelming. Planning became difficult. Certainty disappeared. Yet something unexpected happened in the middle of that instability. Spiritual clarity increased as physical stability decreased. When the body weakened, the inner life grew louder.

People began reaching out. Messages came from those struggling emotionally, spiritually, and mentally. Conversations carried depth without effort. Words came naturally, even when energy did not. The slower life became physically, the clearer purpose felt internally. Compassion deepened. Listening improved. Empathy grew. Pain that once felt isolated became connective.

That truth reshaped everything. Healing did not arrive instantly. Stability did not fully return. Yet grace proved steady. Faith stopped being theoretical. It became practical, daily, and necessary. Trust was no longer about outcomes. It was about presence.

Looking back, every season began connecting. The years in the group home. The heart surgery. The move. The store. College. Vertigo. Each piece fit into a larger picture that only became visible with time. Nothing had been wasted, not the suffering, not the delays, not the weakness.

As the months passed, I became more aware of how deeply this season was reshaping my inner life. Vertigo did not just affect movement; it affected confidence, planning, and identity. Simple things that once required no thought now demanded intention. I could not assume tomorrow would feel like today. That uncertainty forced me to live more honestly in the present. Instead of projecting myself far into the future, I learned to focus on what was possible in front of me.

There were days when frustration pressed hard against my spirit. Watching others move freely, build momentum, and advance in visible ways stirred emotions I had to confront rather than suppress. Comparison tempted discouragement. Questions surfaced quietly but persistently: Why now? Why again? Why after surviving so much already? Those questions did not always receive answers, but they exposed where my trust was still fragile.

During that tension, prayer shifted again. It was no longer focused on outcomes. It centered on endurance. Strength was requested not to escape the situation, but to remain grounded within it. Over time, I noticed something subtle changing. My reactions softened. My expectations adjusted. I stopped measuring progress by speed and started recognizing growth through steadiness.

Scripture continued to meet me in ways that felt personal rather than instructional. Isaiah 40:31 (NIV) speaks clearly into seasons like this: "But those who hope in the Lord will renew their strength. They will soar on wings like eagles; they will run and not grow weary; they will walk and not be faint." That promise did not feel abstract. It described movement at different paces. Some days were for running. Other days were only for walking. And some days required stillness. Yet each pace carried value.

One of the hardest lessons during this time involved releasing the need to explain myself. Limitations often invite misunderstanding. Some people assumed weakness. Others assumed disengagement. I learned that not every season requires explanation. Faithfulness does not always look impressive from the outside. Obedience often unfolds quietly, unnoticed by those who equate value with visibility.

This season also reshaped how I understood leadership. Leadership was no longer associated with authority or influence. It became associated with presence: listening well, responding thoughtfully, and showing consistency even when strength fluctuated. I learned that people do not always need answers. They need space. They need understanding. They need someone who does not rush their process or minimize their pain.

As vertigo slowed my physical pace, it sharpened my emotional awareness. I noticed shifts in conversations. People began sharing deeper truths, not because I sought them out, but because they felt safe doing so. Suffering had created credibility that achievement never could. Pain had taught me how to sit with others without trying to fix them.

Over time, the idea of calling became clearer, though still incomplete. Calling did not feel like a title or role. It felt like responsibility shaped through experience. Everything I had lived through was forming a lens through which I now saw people, systems, and struggles differently. I understood the cost of silence. I understood the impact of fear. I understood the weight of carrying pain privately.

Education continued alongside this growth, but it no longer felt disconnected from life. Concepts had faces now. Theory had stories. Learning felt integrated rather than separate. What once felt intimidating became meaningful. I was not studying to escape my past. I was studying to understand it and eventually use it with wisdom.

There were setbacks along the way: flare-ups that forced rest, days when symptoms intensified unexpectedly, and moments when progress felt reversed. Each setback tested patience. But I learned that setbacks do not erase growth. They reveal how much growth has already occurred. Where panic once ruled, calm began taking its place. Where frustration once dominated, acceptance followed.

Scripture continued grounding me when emotions fluctuated. Psalm 55:22 (NIV) says, "Cast your cares on the Lord and he will sustain you." That verse did not promise the removal of struggle. It promised support within it. Sustaining grace became the theme of this chapter: grace that holds rather than heals instantly, grace that supports rather than resolves completely.

The more time passed, the more I recognized how God was refining priorities. Ambition softened into alignment. Urgency transformed into intentionality. I stopped chasing outcomes and started honoring process. That shift brought relief. It allowed peace to coexist with uncertainty. It allowed trust to grow without demanding control.

Vertigo continued shaping daily life, but it no longer defined it. It became part of the story, not the headline. It taught boundaries. It taught humility. It taught faith expressed through patience rather than performance. That faith did not draw attention, but it built depth.

This chapter represents a long middle season, not crisis, but endurance; not collapse, but reconstruction. These years did not offer dramatic transformation. They offered something quieter and more lasting. They formed character through consistency. They shaped perspective through restraint. They prepared me internally for responsibilities that would later require clarity and steadiness.

During this time, my understanding of life began to shift in ways I did not expect. I stopped measuring forward movement by speed or visible results. Some days looked productive. Others looked quiet and limited. Yet both carried weight. I learned that showing up consistently mattered more than pushing aggressively. Faithfulness began to look ordinary, steady, and intentional rather than dramatic.

I also became aware of how deeply I had tied my identity to action. For years, movement meant safety. Responsibility meant worth. When those things slowed, it exposed how much pressure I had placed on myself to always function at full capacity. Letting go of that mindset was difficult. It required humility. It required honesty. It required accepting that value does not disappear when strength fluctuates.

"The Lord is close to the brokenhearted and saves those who are crushed in spirit" (Psalm 34:18, NIV) became less about emotion and more about presence. Closeness did not feel dramatic. It felt consistent. It felt like being carried through days that offered no clear resolution, but also no abandonment.

I began to recognize that endurance was being formed quietly, not through force or intensity, but through repeated surrender. Some days surrender meant resting without guilt. Other days it meant continuing carefully without pressure. Each choice required trust rather than control.

Stillness became less threatening over time. "Be still and know that I am God" (Psalm 46:10, NIV) stopped sounding like an instruction to stop moving and began to sound like an invitation to breathe. It allowed space for reflection without self-judgment. It allowed trust to grow without urgency.

Pain also sharpened awareness. I became more attentive to what people carried beneath their words. I noticed hesitation. I noticed exhaustion.

I noticed silence. Living inside had taught me how to listen differently. Compassion grew naturally, shaped by experience rather than intention.

The pull toward helping others did not announce itself loudly. It formed quietly through empathy, through patience, through the ability to sit with discomfort without trying to solve it. That capacity was not learned quickly. It was developed slowly, shaped by endurance rather than ambition.

There were days when I questioned whether this season would ever lift. Vertigo remained unpredictable. Uncertainty lingered. But trust did not require certainty. Trust required steadiness. It required believing that even unfinished healing still carried meaning.

CHAPTER 7

WHEN PURPOSE BEGAN TO SPEAK

Starting college as an adult was not something I had ever imagined for myself. For years, I believed that education belonged to a different version of me, a younger version untouched by life's struggles. But after all I had endured, after heart surgery at forty-one, after vertigo and migraines forced my body to slow down, after stepping away from work and reevaluating everything I thought I understood about success, something inside me knew I could not remain where I was.

Returning to school did not feel like ambition. It felt like obedience. There was no excitement about starting over, no confidence that I would succeed, and no sense that I was finally catching up. What I felt instead was urgency. Life had stripped away the illusion that time was unlimited, and the idea of remaining stagnant felt heavier than the fear of failure. Education was no longer about proving intelligence or building status. It felt like survival for the soul. Something inside me knew that growth could not be postponed any longer, even if the path forward was unclear.

The transition was not easy. Walking into education as an adult carried a weight I did not expect. I was surrounded by younger students whose confidence came from a momentum I no longer had. Years of health struggles, pauses, and setbacks made me feel out of place. I questioned whether I belonged in that space at all. Doubt followed me into every assignment, whispering that I was too late, too far behind, and too broken to begin again.

Reading Scripture academically felt uncomfortable in the beginning. I was not used to studying the Bible outside of tradition or ceremony. I was not prepared for the way it would speak to places inside me that were still wounded and unresolved. But the more I read, the more I realized that Christ was not who I had been taught to fear. He was not angry, distant, or waiting to judge. He was patient. He was compassionate. He was close. Each class felt like more than information. It felt like healing. It felt like Christ gently rebuilding everything that had been broken.

For the first time, Scripture was not being used to control or shame me. It was inviting me to heal. As I studied the Bible in an academic setting, I encountered Christ without fear attached to Him. His words did not threaten or condemn; they restored. They challenged me without crushing me. They revealed a God who had not abandoned me in my suffering but had been present even when I could not recognize Him.

Slowly, the resentment I had carried toward faith began to loosen. I was no longer reading Scripture to comply. I was reading it because something inside me was finally safe enough to listen.

She became one of the greatest blessings of that season. She stepped beyond the role of academic guide and became a source of support at a time when my life was still fragile. She called to check on me not just as a student, but as a person. When health challenges threatened to push me out of school, she fought beside me to keep me enrolled. When fear or frustration made me doubt myself, she reminded me that I belonged there. When I wanted to quit, she refused to let me disappear. She helped me register for classes when I was overwhelmed. She made sure I remained connected when vertigo made everything feel unstable. She reached out when I went silent. She believed in the purpose inside me long before I understood it myself.

Her belief arrived during moments when mine felt absent. When vertigo made concentration nearly impossible and fear whispered that quitting would be easier, her voice remained steady. She treated my calling as real even when I doubted it. Her consistency gave me permission to keep going on days when strength felt unavailable.

That kind of support reshaped how I understood encouragement. She did not motivate me with pressure or expectation. She stood with me through instability, reminding me that purpose does not disappear just because circumstances feel heavy. Through her, Christ showed me what steady faith looks like when life feels unpredictable.

As the semesters continued, every class peeled back another layer of who I thought I was. Psychology courses revealed how pain shapes identity. Counseling courses taught me how to listen, to understand people, to see beyond what is spoken. Spiritual formation courses forced me to look at my own heart, my own relationship with Christ, and my own healing.

I found myself writing papers about faith with tears streaming down my face, not because of the assignment, but because I could finally feel Christ drawing me closer. I was not just studying; I was restored. I was not just learning; I was awakened.

Education stopped being something external and became something internal. Lessons followed me beyond assignments and into reflection. Concepts from psychology and counseling mirrored my own story in ways I could not ignore. Pain was no longer something to escape; it was something to understand. Healing was no longer theoretical; it was unfolding slowly inside me.

The more I learned, the more I realized that my experiences were not disqualifications; they were preparation. What once felt like damage began to look like training. Knowledge and faith started working together, not as separate worlds, but as parts of the same calling taking shape.

Pain no longer felt distant or abstract. It felt familiar. I began noticing how many people were surviving quietly, carrying burdens without language or support. Compassion stopped feeling optional; it felt necessary.

My wife and I found ourselves drawn to serve even when our own lives were difficult. We began buying large amounts of food and taking it to homeless shelters. We gathered necessities for people who were living on the streets. We spent nights handing out meals in the cold, not for recognition or pictures or applause, but because something inside us refused to look away. We could not walk past hunger without responding. We could not ignore people sleeping outside without blankets or food. We could not sit comfortably knowing others were suffering. Serving others became the place where we felt the strongest connection to Christ. It became our purpose long before we understood our calling.

Something spiritual was happening beneath the surface. Each time I looked into the eyes of someone who felt forgotten, it felt like something inside me was being restored. Each time I placed food into someone's hands or prayed quietly for a stranger walking away, I felt a sense of purpose I could not explain. It was as if my heart recognized a place I belonged before my mind understood it. I did not feel tired while serving; I felt alive. I felt connected to something greater than myself, something eternal, something that could not be taken away by sickness, weakness, or fear.

One evening, my wife and I stood in a crowded shelter we had delivered food to. Families were lined up shoulder to shoulder. Some held children wrapped in thin blankets. Others watched quietly with eyes that carried years of pain. As I helped distribute meals, a man approached the table slowly. His face looked tired and weathered, and his hands trembled slightly as he reached for his plate. He paused, looked at me, and said quietly, "Thank you. You do not know how much this means."

His voice broke, and tears filled his eyes. For a moment, everything around us faded and time slowed. I felt something shift inside me. It was not pity; it was love. It was a deep, spiritual knowing that this was holy ground, a moment where Christ Himself was present in the exchange, moving between giver and receiver, healing both at the same time.

Purpose does not begin the day you speak publicly or step into a title. Purpose begins the day you choose to care. Ministry begins the moment you love someone enough to help carry their pain. It was never about being ready; it was about being willing. It was never about being perfect; it was about being present. Serving others taught me that calling is not discovered through pride. It is discovered through humility. It is not revealed in strength; it is revealed in weakness. Christ uses the broken to heal the broken. He uses the hurting to comfort the hurting. He uses those who have survived storms to guide those still learning how to stand.

That was the moment I realized ministry had already begun, not someday in the future, not after a degree, not when I felt qualified. It began the moment compassion became the lens through which I saw the world.

It allowed us to see the tears, the hunger, the fear and the desperation in the eyes of people who have waited too long for help. It lit a fire that cannot be extinguished. But every time we packed the medical truck and prayed over the lines of people waiting outside, we knew deep inside that temporary help was not enough.

We knew Christ was calling us to build a place where healing could continue long after we returned home, a place where equipment would stay, where care would be consistent, and where people would be treated not just with medicine, but with love, respect, and compassion. A place where suffering would not be forgotten. I often find myself standing on the land in silence, feeling the wind on my face, envisioning the future that will rise from it.

In those moments, I sense Christ's presence, urging me forward: *Don't stop now. Keep pushing forward. Keep trusting. Keep preparing. Everything I've endured has been shaping me for this moment.* The land is tangible evidence that the future is already unfolding, and it's a reminder that the dream is bigger than mine; it's a responsibility I've been entrusted with, to protect, nurture, and fight for.

Building a clinic is not just about constructing walls and installing equipment. It is about building a place where the hopeless will find strength. It is about creating a space where healing becomes possible again. It is about restoring dignity to people who have been neglected for far too long. It is about showing Christ through action, not just words. And we are not building for ourselves; we have been building for generations. We are building for children who have not yet been born. We are building for families who have been praying for help for years. We are building because suffering should never be normal. We are building because compassion must become structured. We are building because pain needs a place to be treated instead of buried.

The dream is massive. The road is long. The challenges are real. But Christ has never given us a vision without also providing the strength to carry it. Every setback has trained endurance. Every closed door has redirected us to something better. Every battle has strengthened us for what is coming. The land is waiting. The foundation is forming. Faith is maturing. And the vision is moving from hope into manifestation.

We do not have every detail yet, but we are walking by belief, not sight. The clinic will stand. Christ will be glorified. And the same land where suffering has been normal will become the place where miracles are seen.

Yet in the middle of the pressure, there is something sacred. There is a quiet peace that reminds you that the vision did not come from you, and therefore it is not sustained by you. There is a still voice that reminds you that you are not carrying this alone. There is a calm that whispers that what Christ begins, He always completes.

The weight you feel is evidence that you are being trusted with something eternal. It means there is purpose moving beneath the surface even when progress is slow and the fight feels long. It means Christ has chosen you because He already placed inside you what is required to endure. You are not holding the vision; the vision is holding you.

This weight reshaped my understanding of leadership. Strength no longer meant control; it meant surrender. It meant trusting Christ with outcomes I could not manage. Carrying purpose requires humility, patience, and deep dependence.

I learned that purpose does not crush those who carry it with God. It deepens compassion. It sharpens focus. It transforms you into someone who refuses to quit. It teaches the heart to depend on Christ in a way that cannot be learned through comfort. Every step becomes a testimony. Every obstacle becomes training. Every tear becomes an investment. And every breath becomes a reminder that purpose is worth the weight. The vision is bigger than you because it was never meant for just you. It belongs to Christ, and He has trusted you to carry it until it is born into reality.

But through every disappointment, Christ was teaching me a lesson that changed everything. Support does not define calling. Approval does not validate purpose. People cannot stop what God begins. Sometimes Christ allows people to walk away so that you learn to depend on Him instead of them. Sometimes rejection is protection. Sometimes the silence of others is the space where Christ speaks the loudest. And sometimes the absence of help is what builds the strength required to carry the vision without compromise.

The clinic stands as a light in a community that has been overshadowed by years of hardship and limited resources. Many families cannot afford transportation to larger hospitals, and even when they arrive, supplies are often scarce, medications unavailable, and services overwhelmed. The need is overwhelming and urgent. The pain is real and constant. The tears that fall there are not symbolic; they are the cries of mothers praying for their children to survive another night and fathers holding on to hope with everything they have left.

Every time we stand among the people, the reality of suffering becomes impossible to ignore. We see children battling infections that should be simple to treat but become dangerous without care. We see elderly men and women carrying years of silent pain because there is nowhere to go for help. We see young adults facing sickness they should never experience because early care was never available. We see people who wake up believing that survival itself is a victory. Strength is visible everywhere, and hope tries to rise even when life keeps pressing down. Faith becomes the medicine before medicine arrives because prayer is often the only treatment they have ever known.

The mobile clinic showed us the depth of the need. It revealed what statistics could never express and what distance could never allow us to feel. Standing face to face with suffering forces you to respond. It demands movement. It awakens conviction. Watching a mother weep because she finally received antibiotics for her child breaks something inside you. Seeing the relief in a father's eyes when he realizes his family is receiving care becomes fuel that refuses to let the dream die. Those moments do not fade; they become motivation that lives permanently in your heart.

The land where the future permanent clinic will stand is more than soil;

it is sacred ground. It is a place where healing will rise and where dignity will be restored. It is where Christ will use doctors, nurses, volunteers, and servants to do what many believed was impossible. It is where despair will meet hope. When I walk through that land, I can almost hear footsteps entering a building that once existed only as a vision. I can feel the wind moving as if Christ is saying, *Keep going, do not stop; the miracle is already in motion.* The land waits, and so do the people. And we will build.

Sometimes it is in a shelter where someone is fighting to survive another day. The work has shown us that purpose has no borders. It does not stop at a line on a map, and it does not require a passport to be powerful. If Christ sends us, we go. If He places someone in front of us, we help. If He opens a door, we walk through it with faith.

The responsibility is great, but Christ reminds us that we are never carrying it alone. Philippians 1:6 (NIV) says, "being confident of this, that he who began a good work in you will carry it on to completion until the day of Christ Jesus." That promise gives us strength. It steadies our hearts. It reminds us that what Christ starts, He finishes. The assignment will not fail because the vision does not belong to us; it belongs to Him.

Every time we give, we receive something deeper in return. Every time we serve, our purpose grows stronger. Every time we step into the lives of others, we are reminded that we are part of something much greater than ourselves. The dream is not only about a building, even though the clinic will one day stand boldly on the land that waits for it. It is about seeing Christ through hands that serve and through compassion that refuses to give up. It is about proving that love is action, not talk. It is about building something that will outlive us. It is about legacy.

This chapter of the journey reminds us that the assignment is bigger than one location, bigger than one season, and bigger than any single person. It is a calling that stretches across borders and walks into every space Christ instructs us to enter. And as the mission continues to grow, so does the responsibility to protect it, nurture it, and fight for it.

We are not finished. We are only beginning. The vision is alive. The purpose is unfolding. And what Christ started will be completed.

CHAPTER 8

CHRIST REBUILDS A BROKEN FOUNDATION

There comes a moment in every person's life when the foundation beneath them begins to shake. It may happen slowly or all at once, quietly or violently, but the shift is undeniable. It is the moment when everything familiar stops working and the strength we once relied on becomes too weak to hold us up. These seasons do not arrive to destroy us. They arrive to reveal what needs to be rebuilt. Christ sometimes allows everything around us to collapse so that He can show us that the life we built on self-reliance cannot carry the weight of who we are becoming. Real transformation begins when we stop pretending we are unbreakable and acknowledge that something inside us needs healing.

For years, I carried the weight of my past as if survival alone was enough. I believed that if I stayed busy and kept moving, pain would eventually disappear. I convinced myself that I could rebuild my life without depending on anyone, including Christ. I learned how to look strong on the outside while silently falling apart on the inside.

Growing up in a strict Catholic environment, faith was enforced through fear, not relationship. If I did not attend church, I would be punished at school. If I questioned anything, I was corrected harshly. Instead of drawing me closer to God, those experiences pushed me far away. The church became a place of anxiety. God felt distant and unapproachable. Over time, I built walls around my heart, believing it was safer to trust myself rather than a God I could not understand.

Eventually, life exposed the weakness beneath that foundation. Pain has a way of forcing us to face the truth about ourselves. Disappointment, loss, sickness, betrayal, and failure stripped away the image of strength I projected. Survival was no longer enough. I reached a point where my own strength could not support me.

Every part of the life I constructed without Christ began to crumble, and for the first time, I could no longer outrun the emptiness inside me. It was in that broken place that Christ found me, not with anger or judgment, not with rejection, but with patience and grace. He met me at the lowest place and began rebuilding what I had spent years trying to repair on my own.

Healing did not happen quickly. It was quiet. It was uncomfortable. It was slow. Christ began working in the hidden places where no one else could see. He exposed lies I believed about myself and replaced them with truth. He pulled up the roots of shame and planted confidence and identity in their place.

He taught me that worth is not earned. Worth is given. He showed me that surrender is not weakness. Surrender is strength. Rebuilding begins when we stop trying to hold everything together by force and instead allow Christ to reshape us from the inside out.

As Christ rebuilt my foundation, I began to feel purpose stirring deep within me. It was not loud or dramatic. It was a quiet pull in my spirit. I started recognizing that everything I survived was shaping me into someone who could one day help others. Compassion grew where pain once lived.

Hope grew where fear once controlled me. I noticed brokenness in people with a new kind of sensitivity.

I could see myself in their struggles, and instead of turning away, I felt called to step closer. Every time I encouraged someone else, my own healing deepened. Every time I shared part of my testimony, someone else found strength to stand. What once tried to break me was becoming the foundation of my purpose. Christ was turning wounds into wisdom and tears into testimony.

The rebuilding also required separation. As Christ strengthened my foundation, old habits, old mindsets, and old connections began falling away. People who could not go where I was being called slowly drifted from my life. Opportunities that once excited me no longer aligned with where Christ was leading me. At first, the process felt painful.

I felt alone and misunderstood. Later, I realized that separation was not rejection. It was direction. Christ was protecting what He was building inside me. He was clearing space for something greater. Not everything that begins with us is meant to finish with us. Some seasons end because purpose requires room to grow.

Purpose demands responsibility. If Christ was rebuilding me, then I could no longer live from a place of survival. I had to step into discipline and maturity. I learned that calling is not built on talent but endurance. Many people have dreams, but few are willing to endure the process required to carry them. Purpose always costs something.

It requires sacrifice, consistency, and the willingness to walk alone when necessary. I began learning how to choose direction instead of emotion and commitment instead of convenience. The more I surrendered control, the more peace I felt. The more I trusted Christ, the more clarity came. Life stopped feeling chaotic. Everything began to align with intention.

Confidence replaced doubt. Peace replaced fear. Strength replaced insecurity. I could feel Christ guiding every step forward. The rebuilding process was reshaping me into someone I had never imagined I could become. I began to understand that Christ was not rebuilding me simply to repair damage. He was rebuilding me to prepare me. Nothing I lived through was wasted. Every hardship was training. Every delay was preparation. Every prayer was positioning me for the future.

Philippians 1:6 (NIV) says, "being confident of this, that He who began a good work in you will carry it on to completion until the day of Christ Jesus." That truth became the steady place where I rested. Christ does not begin something and walk away. He finishes what He starts. Christ was building endurance in me, not through comfort but through challenges that demanded perseverance. I started to appreciate the process rather than curse it.

The most powerful transformation happened when I stopped trying to rebuild myself and finally allowed Christ to rebuild me from the inside out. For years, I tried to be strong by pretending nothing affected me. I hid the pain. I hid the fear. I hid the insecurity behind silence and isolation.

That silence felt like protection, but it became a prison. It kept me from growing, from trusting, from healing. When I finally surrendered control, everything changed. I learned that real healing begins where pride ends. I learned that Christ cannot fill hands that are clenched tight around self-reliance. When I released what I thought strength was, I discovered what strength truly is. Christ rebuilt what life tried to destroy, not with quick fixes or emotional shortcuts, but with restoration that reached into the deepest places I had avoided for years.

One of the scriptures that anchored me during that time was 1 Thessalonians 5:24 (NIV): "The one who calls you is faithful, and He will do it." That verse was more than inspiration. It became a lifeline. It reminded me that I was a work in progress, not a finished product. Christ was not done with me, even when I felt unfinished and unqualified.

The transformation taking place inside me began quietly reshaping the course of my life, working beneath the surface where no one else could see the progress, but where Christ was strengthening the structure of my identity. What I once viewed as brokenness was slowly revealing itself as preparation. Every piece of my past that I wished I could erase began to carry meaning.

I started recognizing that nothing in my story was wasted. The pain I once resented had created depth. The storms I survived had built resilience. The loneliness had sharpened spiritual awareness. Life itself was teaching me that Christ does not rebuild by restoring what was lost. He rebuilds by constructing something stronger than what existed before.

Moving forward requires more than desire. It required a willingness to face resistance that came from every direction. The closer I stepped toward purpose, the more intense the internal and external pressure became. It was as if everything that once remained quiet suddenly rose up to oppose the progress taking place. Old memories resurfaced and whispered that I was still unqualified.

Thoughts I believed had been conquered returned, trying to convince me that nothing had changed. The enemy works hardest when he knows transformation is becoming reality. He does not waste energy attacking someone who has nothing ahead. His strategy is to exhaust those who are rising so they never fully step into what they carry.

There were moments when I felt surrounded, not by people, but by invisible weight pressing against my spirit. A heaviness settled over my mind at times without warning. Fatigue tried to steal focus. Confusion tried to cloud clarity. Opportunities that once seemed open suddenly looked distant. It felt as if every step forward triggered a pushback designed to make me quit. But something inside had changed.

I was no longer afraid of pressure. Instead of collapsing, I started recognizing that pressure was evidence of progress. If the enemy was fighting this hard, then something powerful must have been forming ahead. That realization became fuel. It gave strength to stand in moments when giving up would have been easy.

The battle revealed how much endurance had been built through years of struggle. I could stand longer than before. I could breathe through fear instead of running from it. Challenges that once felt impossible no longer held the same authority. Purpose demanded discipline, not emotion. It demanded consistency, not excitement. It demanded faith that refused to retreat. The deeper Christ worked within me, the more unshakable I became. A quiet fire burned inside, and no amount of spiritual resistance could extinguish it.

It became clear that the calling ahead required spiritual maturity. Purpose cannot be sustained by emotion or momentary motivation. It must be carried with endurance and conviction. I had to decide that quitting was not an option and retreat was not on the table. I had come too far to return to who I once was.

Christ had invested too much in my growth for me to surrender the progress because of temporary discomfort. I began embracing the process instead of resisting it. I began thanking God for stretching me instead of asking Him to rescue me from stretching moments. Strength was being built in areas of my life that once collapsed easily.

What surprised me most was the peace that settled in the middle of the battle. A calmness emerged that did not come from circumstances improving but from confidence that Christ was in control. That peace became a weapon. It silenced fear. It weakened the enemy's strategy.

It reminded me that the foundation built by Christ cannot be shaken. Pressure could not destroy me. Pain could not break me. Delay could not deny me. Nothing could cancel what Christ had already started. The rebuild was proof that I was being prepared for something with eternal weight.

The more I leaned into purpose, the more I recognized that this journey was never meant to be comfortable. Calling demands sacrifice. Purpose demands refinement. Growth demands pruning. Breakthrough demands resistance. Destiny demands separation from anything that weakens focus or dilutes vision.

To become who Christ intended me to be, I had to release parts of myself that no longer belonged to my future. Letting go was painful, but remaining the same would have been far more costly. Transformation required leaving behind the version of me that was only built to survive. Purpose required stepping into the version of me created to lead.

Leadership did not arrive with a title or a position. It started quietly, long before anyone recognized it externally. It began with the realization that people were watching how I responded to life. They watched how I carried pressure, how I handled disappointment, and how I stood through storms that would have broken me in earlier seasons. Without trying, I became someone others looked to for strength.

People began asking for advice not because I had all the answers, but because they sensed something in my spirit that felt steady. There was a time when I was desperate to fit in, but now I realized I was not created to blend into the background. Christ had set me apart for something that required visibility, courage, and responsibility.

Influence does not always announce itself with applause. It begins quietly, in moments when someone opens their heart because they feel safe in your presence. It begins when a person says, *You helped me without even knowing it.* It begins when someone finds the courage to keep going simply because they watched you refuse to give up. Leadership is not about being seen. It is about being felt.

It is about showing others that survival is possible, that recovery is real, that strength is born through struggle. It is about demonstrating that pain is not the end, but the birthplace of purpose.

There were days I wondered how someone like me could ever lead. I remembered the boy who sat alone in the corner of a cafeteria. I remembered the teenager who avoided speaking because of embarrassment. I remembered the young man who worked quietly in the shadows, believing he was invisible. I remembered every moment when I felt inadequate and unworthy.

Yet now people trusted me, sought guidance, and looked to me as an example. The very parts of my story I once tried to hide had become the very reason people connected with me. Weaknesses had transformed into strength. Silence had transformed into voice. Pain had transformed into purpose.

The more I stepped into that reality, the clearer the calling became. It was not my accomplishments that gave me influence. It was my scars. People followed authenticity, not perfection. They trusted real stories, not polished performances. They were drawn to someone who understood the valley because he had walked through it, not someone who pretended every part of life was easy.

Christ does not choose the strongest according to the world's standards. He chooses the ones who know what it means to depend on Him. He chooses the ones who survived what should have destroyed them. He chooses the ones who can look into brokenness and recognize possibility.

Leadership demanded a deeper level of surrender. It meant being willing to walk ahead even when the path was unclear, knowing that others were following behind. It meant continuing to grow even when growth was painful. It meant letting go of pride, fear, and the need for approval. It meant choosing discipline when comfort was tempting.

It meant becoming someone who could carry the weight of responsibility without collapsing under pressure. Leadership is not glamorous. It is costly. It requires sacrifice. It demands faith. It stretches capacity. It reveals character. But it also unlocks purpose in a way nothing else can.

As I embraced that call, the vision inside me expanded. I began to see beyond my own journey. I saw people who needed someone to fight for them. People who needed someone to speak life into their hopelessness. People who needed someone who could stand beside them in silence without judgment. People trapped in the same darkness I once knew intimately. The thought of leaving them behind felt impossible. Christ did not rebuild me so that I could walk away quietly. He rebuilt me so that I could return to places where others were still fighting battles I had survived and lead them out.

What was once personal became a mission. What was once individual became collective. What was once private now carried responsibility. My life was shifting from internal preparation to external assignment. The foundation was set and tested. The construction phase was complete. Strength was now ready to be used, not hidden. The stirring I felt inside me became too strong to ignore, and I realized that Christ was preparing me for more than personal healing.

What He restored within me was not meant to stay private. It was meant to be lived out publicly with courage. The vision inside my spirit grew clearer and heavier at the same time, as if the weight of purpose was settling into place with undeniable clarity. I understood that everything I had survived was preparation for responsibility.

The brokenness of my past had become the blueprint for compassion, and the seasons of silence had become training grounds for endurance.

Christ was calling me to stand not just for myself, but for others. That kind of calling requires more than motivation. It requires surrender. It requires trust. It requires a willingness to step forward without needing guarantees.

Unexpected challenges surfaced. I began to notice that whenever a person is close to transformation, the enemy fights hardest. He attacks identity, confidence, clarity, and peace. He tries to convince us that we are not worthy, not prepared, and not capable. He whispers that the past disqualifies us and that failure is inevitable. It became clear that the battles I was facing were not random.

They were strategic attempts to stop the very thing Christ was building. Purpose attracts warfare, and warfare reveals who we trust. Instead of collapsing, I learned to stand. Instead of retreating, I learned to pray with conviction. Instead of fearing the battle, I learned to recognize it as confirmation that I was moving in the right direction.

Strength began to rise in places where fear once lived. Peace settled where anxiety once choked me. Confidence grew in areas where doubt once controlled me. It was not the confidence of personal ability. It was the confidence that comes from knowing that if Christ leads the journey, nothing can stop it. I learned that purpose does not require the absence of fear. It requires the decision to move despite it.

I learned that healing is not the end of the story. It is the beginning of transformation. I learned that when Christ rebuilds a life, He does it with intention, detail, and divine timing. What felt like broken pieces were never wasted. They were being arranged into something whole and powerful.

Everything in my life began aligning around that truth. I could not deny that a call was rising inside me. I could not ignore the pull toward helping others find hope. I could not silence the voice in my spirit telling me that survival was no longer enough. I was being called to lead.

I was preparing to speak. I was being shaped to serve. And for the first time, I felt ready. The fear that once controlled me became fuel. The pain that once weakened me became testimony. The silence that once haunted me became wisdom. The foundation Christ built was unshakeable, and every part of me knew that the time to step forward had come.

What came next would require everything I had learned. It would demand resilience, focus, discipline, and faith. It would call me to stand publicly in places where I once hid quietly. It would challenge me to trust Christ beyond what was comfortable and step into an assignment that carried weight far greater than anything I had ever imagined. But I was ready. Ready not because I was strong, but because Christ had become my strength. Ready not because I had all the answers, but because I finally trusted the One who does.

The foundation Christ built in me began to feel steady in a way I had never known before. It felt solid beneath my feet, like standing on ground that could no longer be shaken by storms. Strength was rising quietly within me, not loud or dramatic, but calm and unbreakable.

There was no turning point that announced itself like a spotlight. It was a gradual awakening, the kind that grows through endurance and patience until one day you realize you are no longer the same person you once were. I could feel a deeper clarity guiding my steps, something steady and unforced. The weight I once carried with shame no longer defined me. It became evidence that I had survived what should have destroyed me.

Conversations with people began to show me that something significant was changing inside. People opened up, often without knowing why. They talked about their pain, their disappointments, and silent battles. They trusted me with the truth they hid from the world. I did not ask for those moments. They simply came, and I listened.

I could feel Christ using what I had lived through to help others breathe again. Nothing about it was planned or rehearsed; it happened naturally. It became clear that compassion was not a weakness. It was strength earned through suffering. It allowed me to see people not for what they showed the world, but for what they were carrying inside.

One day I realized something remarkable. I no longer prayed asking to escape the past. I prayed asking how to use it. The pain that once felt like punishment had transformed into understanding. The silence that once felt like abandonment had become a classroom. The battles that once felt unbearable had become training for something greater. Without realizing it, Christ had shaped resilience in places where fear once ruled. I began to see that every tear watered the soil of the future He was preparing.

There is a promise that became an anchor during that time, one I held close when everything around me felt uncertain. In Isaiah 43:2 (NIV), it is written, "When you pass through the waters, I will be with you, and when you walk through the fire, you will not be burned." Those words became proof that survival was never an accident. Christ was present even when I felt alone. He was guiding me even when I felt lost. He was protecting me even when I did not understand the battle I was in.

Life began to take shape differently. Confidence returned, not the loud kind that tries to prove something to the world, but the steady kind that comes when Christ becomes your strength. Fear no longer controlled my decisions. Doubt no longer silenced my voice. I stopped trying to rewrite the past and started preparing for the future. The man who once struggled to stand was now ready to walk with intention. What once felt like broken pieces now fit together into a design crafted with purpose and precision by the hands of Christ.

Every step forward carried meaning. Every day felt like preparation. Every breath felt like grace. The season of rebuilding was complete and the foundation beneath me was strong enough to carry the weight of what was coming. I knew deeply and without hesitation that life was shifting into a different season, one that required boldness, obedience and trust. Not because I was strong, but because Christ had proven Himself faithful through every trial.

Growth is never loud in the beginning. It unfolds in quiet places where no one is watching, where progress feels invisible, and where people often assume nothing is happening. That hidden season became the most defining period of my life. It was in the stillness that Christ strengthened my character, sharpened my vision, and prepared me for responsibility.

The quiet became sacred. It became the place where I learned to breathe again, where I learned patience, and where I discovered the difference between wanting change and being ready for change. I began to understand that rushing would have destroyed what God was building, and that real transformation demands time. A strong foundation is not the result of speed, but of consistency.

Looking back, I see now that Christ was training my spirit to endure weight I once could not have carried. He was teaching me to remain steady when storms raged and to stay confident when nothing around me provided reassurance. He was shaping my heart to remain compassionate even after disappointment. He was preparing me to speak life into others without losing myself in their pain.

Nothing about the journey was accidental. Every step was intentional, every experience was part of a larger design, and every season was necessary. I learned that destiny is not discovered on mountaintops, but earned in valleys. The strongest people are not those who have never fallen. They are the ones who refuse to stay down.

The more time I spent reflecting on what Christ had done, the more I began to appreciate the beauty of slow transformation. Healing is rarely immediate. It grows quietly, like roots beneath the surface, invisible but essential. It strengthens long before it blossoms. I learned to value patience, to stop judging myself for progress that did not move fast enough, and to celebrate small victories that once felt insignificant. Even small steps forward held power. Even silent progress carried evidence of divine movement. Surviving a season that should have broken me became proof that God was with me all along.

Nothing from my past was wasted. Every tear carried purpose. Every battle held instruction. Every loss created space for something greater. Every disappointment redirected me toward alignment rather than defeat. I stopped wishing the story had been different and began thanking God that He never allowed me to quit. The foundation Christ built was not formed from perfection. It was built through survival, courage, endurance, and grace. It was shaped through fire rather than comfort. And because it was forged through struggle, it became unshakable.

CHAPTER 9
THE STEP FORWARD

Healing prepares the heart, but purpose always requires movement. After years of breaking, rebuilding, learning, and surrendering, I reached a point where remaining still was no longer an option. There was nothing dramatic about the moment. No surge of excitement. No sense of triumph. Instead, it came as a quiet but persistent conviction that refused to fade, no matter how much I tried to focus elsewhere. Christ was calling me beyond survival. The season of restoration had accomplished what it was meant to accomplish, and now obedience was asking me to move.

Movement demanded a decision that could not be undone. Once I acknowledged what Christ was asking, there was no neutral ground left to stand on. Remaining where I was would no longer be rest; it would be resistance. I understood that obedience was not simply about starting something new, but about accepting that certain versions of my life were ending. The step forward carried permanence. What I chose next would shape not only my direction, but my identity.

I felt the weight of that reality before I felt excitement. Moving forward meant risking misunderstanding, financial uncertainty, and exposure. It meant stepping into responsibility without guarantees, without applause, and without a clear picture of how everything would unfold. The safety of preparation was giving way to the vulnerability of action. Christ was not inviting me into comfort. He was inviting me into trust.

For the first time, obedience required visible action. It was no longer enough to sense direction internally or carry conviction quietly. I had to begin aligning my schedule, my priorities, and my decisions with what Christ was forming. That meant changing how I spent my time, how I stewarded my energy, and how I responded to opportunities that once felt harmless. Small choices suddenly carried spiritual weight. Obedience became practical, not just personal.

This shift exposed how often I had confused preparation with obedience. Preparation felt productive without being risky, while obedience demanded movement even when clarity was incomplete. I realized that waiting indefinitely for certainty was another form of delay. Scripture had already made that truth clear: "Trust in the Lord with all your heart and lean not on your own understanding; in all your ways submit to Him, and He will make your paths straight" (Proverbs 3:5–6). Christ was not asking me to understand everything. He was asking me to trust Him enough to move with what I had already been given.

That realization did not arrive with a voice from heaven or a sudden clarity that explained everything at once. It unfolded slowly through patterns that became impossible to ignore. People began opening up to me without prompting, trusting me with stories they had not shared elsewhere. Conversations deepened naturally, often drifting toward pain, loss, and quiet battles that were usually kept hidden. Again, I heard the same truth expressed in different ways. People told me they felt seen, that they felt understood, that something in my presence helped them breathe again.

I began to recognize that what I had survived was no longer just my story. Christ was using it to reach others. I started to understand that God does not waste anything. He does not waste pain, silence, disappointment, or years that feel lost. Every tear becomes part of preparation, and every delay becomes material for purpose. Calling is not about position or visibility. It is about responsibility. It is about standing with people who feel crushed and reminding them they are not alone. Purpose does not require a platform. It requires obedience.

The moment I acknowledged that truth, resistance followed. Insecurities I thought had been settled resurfaced unexpectedly. Fear found its voice again, and the past tried to speak louder than the present. Doubt reminded me of every failure, every weakness, and every reason I once believed I was unqualified. The enemy attempted to turn vulnerability into disqualification, suggesting that my history made me unusable rather than prepared. But something inside me had changed. I was no longer willing to agree with those lies.

Courage did not arrive fully formed. It grew slowly as obedience was practiced. Each time I refused to retreat, strength took root. Each time I chose truth over fear, peace settled more deeply. I began to understand that Christ does not call the qualified. He qualifies those He calls. My responsibility was not to feel ready. It was to move forward, trusting that Christ would supply what I lacked.

Stepping into purpose required confronting identities I had carried for years. I had to let go of versions of myself shaped by pain and silence. I had to release the belief that my voice did not matter and stop shrinking to make others comfortable. I could no longer treat my testimony as something to hide. Christ had not rebuilt me so that I could remain silent.

Once my voice entered the space Christ was opening, I could no longer control how it would be received. Some would misunderstand my intent. Others would project expectations I never asked for. I realized that purpose does not only reveal calling; it exposes boundaries. I would have to learn when to speak, when to remain quiet, and when obedience meant refusing roles others tried to assign me.

I also understood that stepping forward would require accountability. I could no longer drift spiritually or emotionally without consequence. Obedience demanded consistency, not intensity. The margin for distraction narrowed. Christ was not just shaping what I would do; He was establishing how I would live under responsibility.

Strength for that season came from a truth I held onto daily. Scripture reminded me that courage is not the absence of fear, but the decision to trust God in its presence. I learned that Christ equips before He releases. He does not send us forward unguarded. He walks ahead of us, stands beside us, and remains with us at every step. Moving forward was never about perfection. It was about obedience. It was about trusting that Christ saw something in me worth using, even when I struggled to see it myself. The story I once wished I could erase was becoming the very message Christ intended me to carry.

Purpose also began requiring separation. Environments that once felt normal no longer supported growth, and voices that weakened faith had to be released. Relationships tied to earlier seasons could not follow me into what was forming ahead. Losing people was painful, but alignment required it. Separation was not rejection. It was direction.

Some separations were immediate. Others unfolded slowly, marked by distance rather than confrontation. Conversations became shorter. Invitations stopped coming. Familiar support systems shifted without explanation. I had to resist the urge to interpret silence as failure. Christ was teaching me that alignment sometimes feels lonely before it feels peaceful.

Letting go was not dramatic, but it was painful. I grieved connections that had once sustained me, even when I knew they could not follow me forward. Purpose did not erase attachment. It required maturity within it.

I learned that obedience does not numb loss; it teaches you how to carry it without turning back.

Even as courage strengthened, life did not become easier. Pressure increased, resistance increased, and distractions multiplied. There were nights filled with tears and mornings filled with questions. Still, quitting was no longer an option. Christ had proven Himself faithful too many times for retreat to make sense.

That tension reshaped my prayer life. I stopped asking Christ to remove pressure and began asking Him to strengthen me beneath it. When that shift occurred, clarity followed. Pain was no longer punishment. It was preparation. The weight was not meant to break me. Each battle refined wisdom, each disappointment taught grace, and each lonely moment deepened dependence on Christ.

I anchored myself in the truth that Christ finishes what He starts. If He placed purpose inside me, He would carry it to completion. That promise became solid ground when confidence felt thin. I realized I was not walking toward something unknown. I was stepping into something Christ had prepared long before I recognized it.

I recognized that obedience has a way of closing doors behind you, even when you hesitate at the threshold ahead. Familiar rhythms could no longer hold the weight of what Christ was awakening within me. Stepping forward was not only about accepting a calling; it was about releasing the comfort of what I had outgrown.

Obedience demanded discipline. It required saying no when yes would have been easier, remaining silent when defending myself felt justified, and continuing forward when motivation disappeared. Purpose was not sustained by emotion; it was sustained by commitment. Opposition often appeared internally rather than externally. Thoughts questioned timing, memories resurfaced to weaken resolve, and old insecurities tried to disguise themselves as wisdom. Yet every attempt to hesitate revealed that hesitation itself had become disobedience.

Forward was no longer optional. Spiritual resistance intensified in subtle ways. Fatigue settled deeper than physical exhaustion, and pressure lingered quietly in the background. The enemy no longer relied on chaos but on persistence, attempting to wear me down rather than stop me suddenly. Obedience reshaped my identity. I became less driven by approval and more anchored in alignment. I stopped explaining myself to those committed to misunderstanding me.

Clarity came not from convincing others but from remaining faithful to Christ. Pressure revealed what had truly changed within me. Situations that once triggered panic now required prayer. Challenges that once caused retreat now demanded endurance. I did not respond perfectly, but I responded differently, and that difference mattered.

Leadership was no longer about visibility or authority. It was about responsibility and consistency. People were watching how I handled pressure, not how loudly I spoke. They noticed how I remained grounded during uncertainty and how I carried myself during delay. Leadership began forming quietly, shaped by integrity rather than ambition.

Choices carried consequences I could no longer ignore. What I allowed into my life, what I tolerated, and what I refused now shaped more than just my own stability. I became aware that obedience creates ripple effects. My faithfulness was no longer isolated; it influenced environments, relationships, and expectations whether I intended it to or not.

That awareness forced me to confront how easily compromise hides beneath good intentions. Not every open door was aligned, and not every opportunity was meant to be accepted. Obedience required discernment that prioritized long-term integrity over short-term affirmation. Christ was teaching me that leadership is not proven by how much you carry but by how wisely you choose what not to carry.

I also became aware of my limitations. I could not be everything to everyone. Obedience required restraint as much as availability. Christ was teaching me that sustainable leadership depends on knowing when to engage and when to step back. Carrying purpose meant protecting clarity, not chasing relevance.

Christ was preparing me to influence without striving. Obedience did not remove uncertainty, but it changed how I carried it. I stopped demanding full understanding before taking the next step because Scripture reminds us that "we live by faith, not by sight" (2 Corinthians 5:7). I also stopped treating unanswered questions as a sign that I had missed God. I learned that faithfulness does not require visibility, only trust.

I learned to recognize the difference between caution and hesitation. Caution brings peace and clarity, even when the road is narrow. Hesitation brings confusion and delay, even when the direction is already settled. As I practiced moving with Christ, I realized that clarity often meets you after you commit, not before you begin.

Silence also began to feel different. It no longer felt like distance. It felt like training. In quiet moments, Christ exposed what was still fragile in me, not to shame me, but to strengthen me. When pressure rose, I learned to pause instead of reacting. When frustration surfaced, I learned to pray instead of performing. I started paying attention to what was happening inside me because I understood that obedience is not only about the steps I take outwardly; it is also about the spirit I carry while I take them.

As my focus sharpened, I became more protective of what fed my faith and what drained it. I stopped confusing busyness with purpose, and I stopped giving my best energy to distractions that produced nothing but noise. I learned to say no without guilt, and I learned to wait without resentment. Some opportunities looked good, but they were not mine. Some conversations felt urgent, but they were not assigned. Obedience taught me that stewardship includes my time, my attention, and my emotional strength.

The weight did not disappear, but I became stronger under it. Responsibility stopped feeling like pressure meant to crush me and started feeling like evidence that Christ trusted me with more. I began to see that faithfulness is the real measure of progress, especially when no one is clapping and nothing looks dramatic. The steps still required courage, but they also required patience, humility, and consistency. That is how I knew I was no longer living to survive. I was learning how to live aligned.

Criticism no longer carried the same weight. Misunderstandings no longer demanded immediate correction. I learned that not every challenge requires defense, and not every accusation requires response. Obedience trained me to protect focus rather than reputation. Peace followed when I allowed Christ to be my defender.

Growth also revealed how obedience reshapes relationships in unexpected ways. Some connections strengthened as values aligned more clearly. Others weakened as priorities shifted. I learned to honor people without allowing attachment to dictate direction. Letting go no longer felt like loss but like alignment. Christ was teaching me that obedience sometimes requires loving people without walking the same path. Yet it was during those ordinary moments that endurance formed.

Faithfulness in repetition built stability. Christ was reinforcing habits that would sustain future responsibility. What felt monotonous was foundational. I also learned that obedience changes how time is perceived. Urgency faded, replaced by intentionality. I stopped rushing outcomes and started respecting process. Each step mattered, even when it seemed small. Patience no longer felt passive; it became active trust. Waiting was no longer a delay but a discipline.

Pressure still existed, but it no longer felt overwhelming. Christ was strengthening my ability to remain steady regardless of circumstance. Stability became the evidence of growth.

Stability revealed something else I had not anticipated. Obedience reshaped how I handled momentum. When progress accelerated, I learned not to rush ahead of Christ. When progress slowed, I learned not to panic. I began to understand that faithfulness is tested not only in hardship but also in seasons of growth. Expansion without grounding can be just as dangerous as stagnation.

Christ was training me to move forward without losing reverence for the process. I stopped equating speed with effectiveness and visibility with fruit. The step forward was not about arriving quickly; it was about remaining aligned regardless of pace. That realization protected me from burnout and preserved the integrity of what Christ was building beneath the surface.

Christ was not only guiding my steps outward but also reshaping how I responded inwardly. Growth began to show itself in restraint, patience, and intentionality rather than impulse. I learned that obedience requires emotional honesty. Acknowledging weariness did not weaken faith; it clarified my dependence on Christ. I began allowing myself to admit when the weight felt heavy without interpreting that honesty as failure. Christ met me consistently in those moments, reminding me that endurance is sustained through honesty, not denial.

Carrying purpose required learning how to protect focus in a world filled with noise. Distractions were not always obvious. Some arrived disguised as good intentions, urgent demands, or unnecessary explanations. Obedience taught me how to discern what required my energy and what did not. I became more selective, not out of pride, but out of stewardship. Compassion grew where frustration once lived. I became more attentive to people's struggles without trying to fix them. Listening replaced advising. Presence replaced pressure. Christ was teaching me that obedience includes how we treat people, not just the direction we walk.

Instead of spiraling, I learned to pause. Prayer became less reactive and more grounding. Silence with Christ became restorative rather than uncomfortable. Trust was no longer dependent on circumstances changing; it was rooted in knowing who was leading.

I stopped anticipating immediate breakthroughs and began valuing gradual progress. Faith matured into something steady and resilient. The desire for quick resolution gave way to appreciation for steady formation. Christ was building endurance that would sustain long-term responsibility. I also became more aware of how obedience challenges control. Surrender required releasing the need to manage outcomes. Trust meant accepting that results were not mine to orchestrate. Each step forward required letting go of the illusion that certainty was necessary for progress. Peace followed when control loosened its grip.

When plans shifted or outcomes disappointed, I no longer interpreted them as failures. I learned to ask what was being shaped rather than what was being lost. Setbacks became moments of refinement rather than reasons to retreat.

Relationships continued evolving as alignment deepened. I learned to release expectations without resentment. Love remained, but dependency faded. Obedience allowed me to remain connected without compromising direction. Healthy distance became an expression of wisdom rather than rejection.

Another shift occurred as obedience shaped discipline. Habits formed quietly. Prayer became consistent rather than situational. Reflection became routine rather than reactive. These disciplines did not feel restrictive; they felt stabilizing. Christ was reinforcing a structure that could support future weight.

I learned how obedience sharpens humility. Recognition was no longer motivating. Approval lost significance. Faithfulness became the goal. Christ was teaching me to serve without needing acknowledgment, to lead without demanding affirmation, and to move forward without needing permission. Endurance strengthened as obedience became habitual. Difficult days no longer disrupted direction. Fatigue no longer dictated decisions. I learned how to rest without disengaging and how to pause without losing momentum. Balance formed through intentional rhythms rather than extremes.

Success was no longer measured by visibility or outcomes. It was measured by consistency, alignment, and faithfulness. Progress became something internal before it was ever external. Christ was prioritizing character over accomplishment. Direction sharpened without force. Trust deepened without explanation. Obedience no longer felt heavy; it felt necessary. The forward path became familiar, not because it was easy, but because it was aligned.

It operated through trust, discipline, and surrender. Christ had reshaped my understanding of strength, redefining it as endurance rather than intensity. The step forward had become more than an action; it had become a posture. Life was no longer approached cautiously. It was approached faithfully. Decisions were made with intention. Direction was maintained with humility. Growth continued without urgency.

When plans did not unfold as anticipated, I resisted the urge to interpret delays as denial. Obedience taught me that timing is part of purpose. What felt postponed was often protected. What felt withheld was often preparation. Trust expanded as I learned to release the urgency for immediate results. Obedience also revealed how deeply pride can hide within good intentions. Christ gently exposed those motives, not to shame me, but to free me. I learned that obedience is not about being seen as faithful; it is about remaining faithful even when unseen.

The longer I walked in obedience, the more responsibility felt internal before it was ever external. I became mindful of how I spoke, how I listened, and how I responded under pressure. Obedience extended beyond actions into attitudes. Integrity mattered more than impression. Consistency mattered more than recognition.

Each season prepared me for the next without overwhelming me prematurely. Looking back, I could see how carefully the process had been measured. Nothing was rushed. Nothing was wasted. Not every invitation required acceptance. Discernment taught me how to remain focused without becoming rigid. Saying no became just as important as saying yes. Both were acts of obedience when guided by alignment.

Rest and discipline began working together rather than competing with one another. Pressure continued to test endurance, but it no longer produced panic. Instead, it revealed stability. When challenges arose, I found myself responding with prayer rather than urgency. Solutions were no longer forced. Trust replaced control. Christ was teaching me how to remain steady without becoming passive.

Doubt still appeared, but it no longer dictated movement. Confidence became grounded, quiet, and resilient. It did not need reinforcement; it simply remained. It begins with how a person carries responsibility when no one is watching. Christ was shaping leadership internally before allowing it to manifest externally.

I stopped expecting immediate growth where healing was still unfolding. Grace deepened as I remembered how long my own transformation had taken. Obedience softened judgment and strengthened empathy. Even setbacks took on new meaning. Rather than discouraging me, they refined me. Each obstacle revealed areas still being strengthened. Each challenge exposed what had already grown. Obedience reframed difficulty as instruction rather than interruption.

It was about trusting Christ's leading regardless of outcome. Faithfulness became the measure. Alignment became the reward. Movement continued, not because clarity was complete, but because trust had matured. The step forward was no longer something I questioned; it was something I experienced. Each day reinforced the decision to remain aligned, disciplined, and faithful. Purpose unfolded not through dramatic moments, but through consistent obedience carried over time.

CHAPTER 10
THE CALL TO SERVE

The call to serve did not enter my life through clarity or certainty, nor did it arrive with the kind of confidence people often associate with purpose. It came quietly, forming beneath the surface while I was still learning how to live with my own healing. At that point, I was not looking to help anyone else, and I was not searching for direction beyond survival and stability.

My attention was still turned inward, learning how to breathe without fear, how to trust my body again, and how to rebuild a life that had been interrupted repeatedly by illness, loss, and unanswered questions. Yet even in that fragile place, people began to find me, not because I presented myself as someone with answers, but because something in my presence felt safe enough for them to speak.

Conversations began unfolding in unexpected ways. What started as ordinary exchanges slowly moved into deeper territory without effort or prompting. People shared fears they had never spoken aloud, grief they had buried for years, and exhaustion that came from carrying life alone without relief. I did not guide those conversations or try to direct them toward resolution.

I listened because listening felt natural, and I stayed because leaving felt wrong. Over time, I began to recognize that these moments were not random. Christ was already at work, using my own history of silence, pain, and endurance to create space where others could finally exhale. I was not offering solutions; I was offering presence, and that presence carried more weight than I understood at the time.

What struck me most during those early moments was how universal suffering revealed itself once people felt seen. Pain did not discriminate based on age, success, education, or appearance. It lived quietly beneath accomplishments and behind practiced smiles.

Many of the people who opened up to me appeared strong on the outside, yet inside they were unraveling under pressure they believed they had to carry alone. When they recognized their own struggle reflected in mine, not through shared details but through understanding, something shifted. They spoke freely, not because I encouraged them to, but because they felt understood without explanation.

Slowly, my understanding of ministry began changing. I had grown up believing that service required structure, permission, or visibility, something official that validated involvement. What I was discovering instead was that ministry often begins in hidden places, long before anyone names it.

It exists in quiet conversations that leave no record and in moments where the only witness is Christ Himself. These moments demanded something deeper than knowledge or preparation. They required patience, restraint, and the willingness to remain present without needing to feel useful. I began to see that Christ was not asking me to perform faith, but to embody it.

As these encounters continued, responsibility increased in ways I had not anticipated. Listening deeply requires endurance, because when people trust you with their pain, that pain does not disappear when the conversation ends. Stories linger. Faces return to memory. Questions remain unresolved.

There were evenings when the emotional weight of what I had heard followed me into silence, pressing against my thoughts long after the moment had passed. That weight forced me to confront something essential: serving others without discernment would eventually break me. Compassion without structure would not last. Christ was beginning to teach me that sustainability is not a lack of faith, but an act of wisdom.

In the beginning, it was tempting to respond to every need immediately. The urgency felt spiritual, and saying yes felt like obedience. Over time, that approach revealed its limits. Exhaustion crept in quietly, not because the work was wrong, but because boundaries were absent.

Christ did not call me to carry everything placed in front of me. He called me to discern what was assigned and release what was not. Learning that difference reshaped my understanding of responsibility. Care does not require control. Presence does not require ownership. Trusting God meant believing that what I could not resolve was never mine to manage.

With that realization, clarity began replacing urgency. I learned to pause before responding, to pray before committing, and to wait without guilt. Decisions felt steadier. Peace followed restraint. I became aware of the difference between exhaustion that comes from obedience and depletion that comes from misalignment. One strengthens. The other drains. That distinction became essential as the work continued because, without it, even sincere service would quietly erode purpose.

Consistency slowly built trust. People returned, not because I promised answers, but because I remained present. They spoke more freely over time, knowing their stories would not be rushed, minimized, or shared carelessly. Confidentiality, reliability, and integrity formed credibility without effort or self-promotion. Leadership emerged quietly through repetition rather than declaration. Showing up consistently mattered more than saying the right thing once. People watched patterns more than words, and those patterns began shaping influence without my awareness.

Responsibility also revealed parts of myself that isolation had hidden. Old insecurities resurfaced. Memories I believed were settled returned unexpectedly. Rather than resisting those moments, I learned to face them honestly. Christ was continuing His work in me even as He worked through me. Service became a refining space where fragility could no longer be ignored. Growth came not through avoiding discomfort but through remaining faithful within it.

Over time, it became clear that this was not a temporary phase or a response to circumstance. It was direction. The call to serve began shaping how I lived, how I listened, and how I moved through daily life. Purpose was no longer something distant or future-oriented. It became embodied in ordinary moments, often unseen and unacknowledged. These moments did not feel dramatic, but they carried weight because they demanded faithfulness without feedback.

One of the hardest lessons during this season involved releasing control over outcomes. Helping others does not guarantee visible change, gratitude, or resolution. Some people grew slowly. Others resisted. Some disappeared without explanation. Early on, these moments tempted discouragement and self-doubt. Christ dismantled that mindset patiently, teaching me that obedience ends where control begins. My responsibility was presence, integrity, and faithfulness, not results. Letting go of outcomes did not reduce responsibility; it clarified it.

As the emotional weight accumulated, rest became necessary rather than optional. Reflection and decompression were no longer luxuries. Without them, compassion would have turned into fatigue, and fatigue into withdrawal. Christ was teaching me that caring for others required caring for the vessel through which care flowed. Ignoring limits would not strengthen the work; it would quietly undermine it. Learning to rest without guilt and pause without retreat preserved clarity and endurance.

Silence began teaching me as much as conversation ever had. Sitting with someone in pain without forcing resolution required trust. Many did not need answers. They needed space. They needed to know they were not a burden for feeling what they felt. Remaining in those moments, even when they felt unfinished, mattered more than speaking well. Faithfulness revealed itself through repetition. Showing up again, especially when nothing seemed to change, formed depth that visibility never could.

Recognition gradually lost its grip on me. Earlier in life, being unseen felt like rejection. In this season, it felt like freedom. Obedience no longer required affirmation. Peace followed when value was measured by alignment rather than response. Responsibility sharpened awareness. Words mattered. Silence mattered. Integrity mattered. Serving others demanded maturity in posture as much as action.

These moments challenged sustainability, wisdom, and long-term faithfulness. Christ met me there, not by removing the weight, but by teaching me how to carry it without strain. Calm replaced reaction. Presence replaced performance. Discernment deepened.

Consistency became the true test. Showing up once required courage. Showing up repeatedly without recognition required resolve. Many nights felt ordinary and quiet, yet those moments mattered more than I realized. They trained steadiness independent of emotion. Commitment replaced excitement. Service became sustainable because it rested on obedience rather than momentum.

Looking back, my life had prepared me for this work. The pain, the waiting, the rebuilding, and the resistance were not detours. They were formation. Each experience sharpened discernment and strengthened endurance in ways comfort never could. Longevity mattered more than speed. Finishing well demanded patience, humility, and discipline.

The call to serve continues to require growth. New challenges emerge. Responsibilities deepen. Lessons continue. Fear no longer dictates my response. Trust has taken its place. I do not need to see every step ahead. I need only remain faithful to the step in front of me. Purpose is sustained not by certainty, but by obedience practiced daily, quietly, and consistently.

I became more aware of how service reshapes the inner life over time. It does not only change how you respond to others; it changes how you relate to yourself. Carrying responsibility consistently forces honesty. It exposes motivations, reveals limits, and removes illusions that survive comfortably in theory but collapse under lived demand.

I began noticing how easily compassion can drift into obligation if awareness is lost, and how obligation, when carried too long, dulls sensitivity instead of deepening it. Christ was teaching me that service requires continual recalibration, not to protect comfort, but to preserve clarity and integrity. Without that recalibration, even sincere intentions can become heavy, and what begins as calling can quietly turn into strain.

The longer I served, the more I understood that faithfulness is measured less by intensity and more by steadiness. Moments of strong emotion were not reliable indicators of direction. Some days felt full and affirming. Others felt quiet, heavy, or unresolved. Yet both demanded the same commitment. Service required showing up when nothing felt exceptional and remaining present when progress was invisible. That discipline formed something deeper than motivation. It formed trust, both within me and in those I served. People did not return because of powerful moments. They returned because consistency created safety, and safety allowed honesty to surface gradually without pressure.

I also began to see how responsibility alters the way time is experienced.

Early on, urgency shaped my responses. Everything felt immediate, and every need seemed to demand attention. Over time, Christ slowed my pace internally, teaching me that not every situation requires instant engagement. Some moments needed patience rather than a response. Some struggles needed time rather than intervention. Learning to wait without withdrawing became an essential discipline. Waiting was no longer passive. It was attentive. It required trust that God was working even when my involvement was limited. That trust freed me from the pressure to always act and allowed discernment to guide my steps more clearly.

Another quiet shift took place as service became part of my daily rhythm. I noticed that people often arrived carrying expectations they did not articulate. Some hoped for answers. Others wanted relief. A few looked for certainty. Learning not to absorb those expectations became necessary. Christ did not ask me to become what people needed in the moment. He asked me to remain faithful to what He assigned. When I attempted to meet expectations that were not mine to carry, confusion followed. When I remained aligned, peace returned. That clarity protected both the work and my spirit, allowing service to remain grounded rather than reactive.

Over time, I also recognized that service has a way of confronting pride in subtle forms, not the obvious kind, but the quiet desire to feel needed, useful, or irreplaceable. Those impulses rarely announce themselves. They hide beneath good intentions and a willingness to help. Christ addressed those areas gently but firmly, reminding me that usefulness does not equal ownership and that being needed should never become a source of identity. The work was never meant to depend on me. It was meant to flow through obedience, humility, and trust. Releasing the need to be central allowed service to remain healthy and sustainable.

The emotional weight of listening continued to require careful attention. Stories carried residue, and some followed me longer than expected. Without intention, those burdens could accumulate quietly. I learned the importance of releasing what was entrusted to me back into God's care rather than carrying it alone. Prayer became less about asking for solutions and more about surrendering what I was not meant to hold.

That practice restored balance. It allowed compassion to remain open without becoming overwhelming. Christ was teaching me that caring deeply does not require carrying endlessly.

As the months passed, patterns emerged. Certain struggles repeated themselves in different lives. Similar fears surfaced through different voices. I learned that growth rarely follows a straight line. People move forward, pause, retreat, and advance again.

Expecting linear progress, with its neat and tidy milestones, created frustration and disappointment, whereas accepting the messy and unpredictable nature of the process, with its ups and downs, allowed me to preserve my endurance and cultivate a deeper sense of resilience and perseverance. I became more patient, less reactive, and more grounded in the understanding that transformation unfolds at different paces. My role was not to accelerate healing, but to remain steady within it.

Service also refined how I communicated. I became more intentional with words, aware that speech carries weight beyond intention. Sometimes restraint communicated care more clearly than explanation. Silence, when offered with presence, created room for others to find their own footing. I learned that wisdom often sounds quieter than urgency and that discernment rarely rushes. This shift did not diminish authority. It deepened it. People felt respected rather than managed, supported rather than directed.

The longer I walked this path, the more clearly I understood that service is not sustained by passion alone. Passion fluctuates. Commitment remains. Faithfulness required structure, boundaries, and rhythm. Without them, even genuine calling becomes unstable. Christ was teaching me to build practices that supported longevity rather than intensity. Rest became intentional. Reflection became necessary. Preparation mattered. These disciplines did not restrict service. They protected it.

When discouragement surfaced quietly, not through crisis but through fatigue, questions emerged about sustainability, effectiveness, and long-term capacity. Those questions were not signs of weakness; they were invitations to deepen trust. Christ met me there, not by removing responsibility, but by reminding me that endurance grows through dependence, not control. The work was never meant to be carried alone. Recognizing that truth restored perspective and renewed clarity.

Over time, service reshaped how I understood leadership. Leadership was not about influence or visibility; it was about reliability. It was about remaining present when things felt repetitive or slow. It was about guarding integrity when no one was watching. Leadership formed through consistency, not assertion. People responded to what was stable, not what was impressive. That realization removed pressure and allowed me to serve without striving.

As this season continued, it became evident that the call to serve would require ongoing growth. Responsibility would increase. Complexity would deepen. Challenges would evolve. But fear no longer held authority. Trust had taken its place. I learned that I did not need to anticipate every demand or prepare for every outcome. I needed to remain attentive, faithful, and aligned. The work would unfold as it was meant to, step by step, without forcing clarity before its time.

The call to serve is not marked by arrival; it is sustained through practice. It unfolds through repetition, humility, and attentiveness to God's leading. It requires endurance that is formed slowly and strengthened through consistency. What began quietly continues quietly, not because it lacks significance, but because faithfulness rarely announces itself. It builds depth before it reveals fruit.

As I look ahead, I no longer feel the urgency I once did. I feel responsibility, clarity, and resolve. Service has become part of how I live rather than something I do. It shapes decisions, relationships, and priorities. It demands awareness and humility. It requires trust that God is working beyond what I can see. Purpose remains grounded not in certainty, but in daily obedience carried with intention.

This calling continues to shape and refine me, even as it expresses itself through my actions and words. It is a journey of ongoing growth, a process of transformation that unfolds slowly over time, without ever reaching a point of completion or finality. It invites me to embrace a path of continuous learning, to surrender to the reality that there is always more to discover, more to understand, and more to become.

Each new day brings with it a fresh opportunity to remain faithful to the journey, to listen attentively to the whispers of God's guidance, and to serve others with humility and compassion, unencumbered by attachment to specific outcomes or expectations. In this surrender, I find a profound sense of peace and purpose, a deepening awareness that this is not about achieving a particular status or accomplishing a specific goal, but about embodying the love and character of Christ in every moment, in every interaction, and in every circumstance.

I am reminded that the call to serve is not a destination, but a journey. It is a journey that requires surrender, trust, and obedience, even when the way forward is unclear. It is a journey that demands humility, compassion, and perseverance, even in the face of uncertainty and doubt. Yet it is in this journey that I have found true fulfillment, a sense of purpose that is not derived from external validation or success, but from the knowledge that I am living out the calling God has placed on my life. I am learning to trust in the goodness and sovereignty of God, to trust in the promise that He is working all things together for my good, even when I cannot see the bigger picture.

In the midst of this journey, I have also come to realize that the call to serve is not just about serving others, but about allowing myself to be served by God. It is about recognizing that I am not alone, that I am part of a larger story, a story being written by the Author of life. It is about learning to receive the love, grace, and mercy of God, and allowing it to transform me, shape me, and use me for His purposes. This is the heart of the call to serve, and it is a call that continues to shape, mold, and transform me into the person God is calling me to be.

CHAPTER 11

THE BATTLE BEHIND
THE CALL

Walking on purpose is not as straightforward as people imagine. When Christ begins to lead you into something greater, the fight does not get easier, it gets heavier. I learned quickly that stepping into what He called me to do meant entering a battlefield. Every time I tried to move forward, something pushed me backward. Every time I gained momentum, resistance appeared. I used to think that following Christ made the path smooth and removed obstacles. Instead, I discovered that obedience attracts warfare. The closer I moved toward what I was created to do, the stronger the attacks became.

Many people see the public moments of ministry, but they do not see the private battles. They hear the message but do not hear the silent prayers spoken between breaths. They read the words but do not feel the weight behind them. They see strength but do not see the nights I sat alone, trying to gather enough courage to keep going. They do not see the moments when dizziness hit so hard the room spun while I was preaching. They do not see the migraines that felt like hammers striking my skull. They see only the finished moment, not the fight behind it.

I cannot count how many times I taught or prayed for others while my own body felt like it was collapsing. There were nights when I could barely stand, yet Christ gave me enough strength to finish. Many times, the screen went black, and I sat in silence afterward, exhausted and shaking. Still, I made it through, not because I was strong, but because Christ carried me when my body could not support itself. I learned that purpose does not wait for comfort. It demands commitment when everything in you wants to quit.

The hardest battles are not the ones people can see. Real warfare takes place in the mind and spirit when no one is watching. Suffering privately while carrying responsibility publicly can feel like living in two different worlds at once. On the outside, I continued to lead, speak, pray, and encourage others. On the inside, discouragement often felt heavier than physical pain. Doubt whispered that I was not strong enough to continue. Leadership can feel lonely, not because people are absent, but because responsibility cannot be shared. You can receive help, but you must carry the weight yourself.

Serving others while battling sickness sharpened my awareness of how deeply people hurt in silence. When vertigo hit without warning, it felt as if the ground shifted beneath my feet. The room would spin even while I stood still, and I held onto whatever I could reach just to remain upright. Migraines blurred my vision until even light felt unbearable. There were moments when I spoke through pain, praying that no one could hear the struggle in my voice. Yet grace met me every time I reached my limit. When I thought I could not continue, Christ carried me through the next breath.

Another layer of battle came from people I expected to support me. Some grew silent without explanation. Others distanced themselves when I needed them most. Churches and leaders I hoped would walk alongside the vision disappeared. Promises were made and not kept. Over time, I learned that not everyone who claps for you is truly standing with you. Their absence was not rejection from Christ; it was separation meant to shift my dependence from people to God.

There were moments when trusting Christ felt like stepping into darkness without knowing what awaited on the other side. Nothing about the journey felt easy, but endurance was formed in the struggle. Every time I chose to continue, something inside me grew stronger. Fear became discipline. Isolation became intimacy with Christ. What once felt like punishment became confirmation that I was moving in the right direction. The enemy does not fight what does not threaten him. The battle itself became evidence of calling.

The scripture that sustained me through many sleepless nights spoke to my spirit like medicine for the soul: "My grace is sufficient for you, for my power is made perfect in weakness" (2 Corinthians 12:9, NIV). Those words anchored me when my body failed and when silence from heaven felt loud. Weakness was not disqualification; it became the place where Christ's strength was revealed.

Every time I finished teaching with trembling hands or blurred vision, gratitude followed. Christ trusted me with His people even while I was broken. He allowed me to serve through pain so others could witness what grace truly looks like. He allowed suffering to give my voice authenticity rather than theory. I remained standing not because of ability, but because of obedience.

Suffering reshaped how I saw people. It taught me to recognize quiet pain and listen without judgment. I stopped seeing brokenness as something to fix and began seeing it as something to stand beside. Compassion was no longer an idea; it was formed through experience.

The clinic that lives in my heart was born from those seasons. It was not created from ambition or recognition. It came from watching people suffer without access to care, from seeing families struggle, and from experiencing sickness in my own body. The vision did not feel optional; it felt assigned. It was never about building something impressive. It was about saving lives and restoring hope.

Christ used pain to teach compassion. Every setback became instruction. Every disappointment provided direction. Every attack served as training. Without sickness, loss, fear, and delay, the clinic would have remained an idea. Suffering transformed it into purpose. Every prayer whispered in the dark prepared me for the light. Every tear carried meaning. Every struggle trained me for responsibility. I am still walking through challenges, but I stand shaped, not defeated.

The loneliness of calling became one of my greatest teachers. Christ did not announce separation. He allowed environments to shift, conversations to change, relationships to fade, and silence to grow loud. That quiet space forced reflection, dependence, and trust. Purpose is not crowded; it is narrow, and much of it must be walked alone.

Silence exposed what activity could hide. It revealed whether my faith was rooted in God or in momentum. In that stillness, I learned to pray without encouragement, believe without proof, and continue without comfort. Strength was built underground long before fruit appeared above the surface.

Leadership changed me internally. It was no longer about speaking well or appearing strong. It became about patience, discipline, and humility. Growth required honesty. Boundaries became necessary. I learned to obey the rest I was called to take. Availability without wisdom led to exhaustion, and Christ did not call me to burn out.

Support, especially from my wife, mattered deeply. Her prayers grounded me when fear surfaced. Her reminders strengthened me when exhaustion whispered quit. That support did not remove the weight, but it helped me carry it. Purpose continued to exist inside real life. Bills still came. Needs still existed. Faith was tested when resources felt limited and the vision remained large.

Some days I encouraged others while wrestling with uncertainty myself. Leaders struggle too. The difference is they keep walking. Galatians 6:9 (NIV) stayed close to me: "Let us not become weary in doing good, for at the proper time we will reap a harvest if we do not give up."

The battle behind the call refined rather than removed the assignment. Pressure strengthened vision. Delay matured purpose. Christ sustained me while still requiring discipline. Impact was not always visible, but obedience was never wasted.

As responsibility continued to grow, I became more aware that calling does not only challenge faith, it challenges discipline. Passion alone could not sustain what Christ was asking me to carry. There were days when desire was present but energy was not, and moments when belief was strong but focus scattered. I learned quickly that without structure, even the strongest convictions begin to weaken. Purpose required order, not emotion. Consistency mattered more than intensity.

I had to confront habits that once felt harmless but now interfered with endurance. Poor sleep, unmanaged stress, and constant availability slowly eroded clarity. I realized that obedience includes caring for the body, managing time, and protecting attention. Neglecting these areas did not make me more spiritual; it made me more vulnerable. Christ was not asking me to sacrifice wisdom. He was asking me to steward responsibility.

This season exposed how easily people confuse faith with neglect. I once believed pushing harder was proof of commitment. Over time, I learned that wisdom often requires restraint. Rest was not optional, it was necessary. Not resting did not prove strength; it revealed imbalance. I had to learn that stewardship includes knowing when to stop, pause, and recover. Without recovery, calling becomes distortion instead of assignment.

Responsibility also reshaped how I viewed leadership. Leadership was no longer about vision alone, it became about sustainability. It was no longer enough to know where I was going; I had to learn how to get there without collapsing along the way. This required patience with myself, honesty about limits, and humility to adjust when something was not working. Growth demanded correction, not denial.

I also learned that leadership exposes emotional patterns that pressure reveals. Stress did not create impatience; it exposed it. Fatigue did not create frustration; it uncovered it. When pressure increased, unresolved areas surfaced quickly. This forced me to confront reactions I once excused. Maturity required accountability, not justification. I could not lead others well while ignoring areas that needed attention within myself.

Another lesson came through disappointment that did not resolve quickly. Some prayers were not answered within the timeframe I expected. Some doors remained closed longer than I believed they should. This tested my understanding of trust. I had to accept that faith is not agreement with God's timing, it is submission to it. Waiting did not mean stagnation; it meant preparation. The delay was not punishment; it was positioning.

During this time, I began to understand how easily comparison can undermine purpose. Seeing others advance more quickly was distracting. Their success was not my failure, and their pace was not my assignment. Comparison did not motivate me; it weakened clarity. Letting go of comparison was difficult, but necessary. The work Christ placed before me required full attention, not divided focus.

I also learned that responsibility shapes communication. Speaking impulsively under pressure created confusion. Silence, when used wisely, protected relationships. Listening became more important than responding.

Not every situation required explanation; some required understanding. Leadership demanded discernment in speech, not volume. Words carried weight, and careless language caused unnecessary damage.

Expectations increased as consistency became visible. Some were reasonable; others were not. I had to accept that meeting every expectation was impossible. Boundaries became essential. Saying no was not rejection; it was protection. Without boundaries, calling becomes diluted. With boundaries, purpose remains focused. This lesson was uncomfortable but necessary for longevity.

Financial responsibility also brought a unique kind of pressure. Purpose exists within real life, bills do not disappear because calling is present, and vision still requires resources. Faith was tested when provision felt delayed and responsibilities persisted. I had to learn how to remain disciplined financially without allowing stress to dictate decisions. Stewardship mattered; panic did not. Planning did.

There were moments when I encouraged others while privately wrestling with uncertainty. This revealed another truth: leaders struggle too. The difference is not the absence of doubt; it is the refusal to quit. Leadership does not eliminate fear. It teaches you how to move forward despite it. That distinction reshaped how I understood strength.

I also became more aware that impact is not always immediate. Some seeds grow quietly, and some results appear long after effort is applied. Obedience does not always provide instant feedback. This tested patience deeply. The temptation to measure effectiveness by visible results had to be resisted. Faithfulness mattered more than recognition.

This season also required emotional honesty. Pretending everything was fine did not strengthen faith; it weakened it. Christ did not ask me to perform stability, He asked me to pursue truth. Naming fatigue allowed correction. Acknowledging pressure allowed adjustment. Ignoring reality did not protect calling; facing it did. Over time, my definition of success changed. Success was no longer speed; it was sustainability. It was not expansion; it was endurance. It was not recognition; it was obedience. Being able to continue mattered more than being noticed. Remaining grounded mattered more than appearing impressive.

The weight did not disappear, but my response matured. What once felt overwhelming became manageable through discipline, prayer, and structure. Pressure no longer dictated decisions; purpose guided them. The battle behind the call did not weaken me; it clarified me. I began to recognize that Christ was preparing me not only for what I could see but also for what I could not yet imagine. Responsibility increased as capacity grew. The process was uncomfortable but necessary. Depth was being formed where surface strength would not survive.

Looking ahead, I understand that this season was foundational. What was built here will support everything that follows. Nothing learned was accidental. Nothing endured was wasted. The battle behind the call shaped the strength required to carry the future without breaking.

Before this season, I believed identity was something you discovered once and then carried forward unchanged. I thought that knowing who I was in Christ would remain steady regardless of circumstance. What I learned instead is that responsibility exposes whether identity is rooted in truth or supported by conditions. When pressure increased and comfort disappeared, I could no longer rely on former definitions of strength. I had to confront who I was becoming, not just who I believed myself to be.

This process was uncomfortable because it forced me to release versions of myself that no longer fit the weight I was carrying. Certain habits, expectations, and self-perceptions that once felt acceptable began to feel misaligned. I realized that calling does not simply assign work, it reshapes the person carrying it. That reshaping is rarely dramatic. It happens quietly, through repeated decisions, uncomfortable adjustments, and the steady realization that the old way of functioning is no longer sustainable. Growth required releasing familiarity and accepting transformation without fully understanding the final version.

Responsibility also revealed how deeply I valued control. I wanted clarity before commitment, reassurance before obedience, and certainty before moving. But calling does not operate that way. It demands action before explanation and trust before evidence. I had to confront how often I tried to manage outcomes rather than remain faithful to instruction. Letting go of control did not happen all at once; it happened gradually, as I recognized that attempting to control what I could not govern only increased frustration and anxiety. Surrender was not passive, it was active trust, practiced daily.

Another shift occurred in how I understood faith. Faith was no longer an emotional posture or a confident declaration. It became a discipline of consistency, showing up in routine decisions, unseen obedience, and steady follow-through when no emotional reinforcement was present. I learned that faith matures when it no longer depends on how inspired you feel. It becomes reliable when it operates regardless of internal conditions. That kind of faith is quieter but far stronger. It does not collapse under pressure because it is not built on enthusiasm.

Calling also forced me to confront how I handled disappointment. Earlier in life, disappointment often felt personal. Delays felt like rejection, and closed doors felt like judgment. In this season, I began to understand that disappointment is not always denial. Sometimes it is protection. Sometimes it is timing. Sometimes it is redirection that cannot be explained until much later. Learning to live with unresolved disappointment without allowing it to poison obedience required maturity I had not possessed before this chapter of my life. That maturity was developed slowly through prayer, reflection, and repeated choices to remain steady.

I also began to see how responsibility affects relationships in subtler ways than separation alone. Even when people remained present, dynamics shifted. Conversations became more guarded. Expectations changed. Assumptions formed. I learned that leadership requires discernment not only about who walks with you, but also about how close they are allowed to walk. Access is not entitlement. Proximity must be earned through trust, understanding, and alignment. This was not about distancing myself emotionally; it was about protecting clarity and peace so responsibility could be carried effectively.

Another reality emerged regarding vulnerability. I once believed vulnerability meant sharing everything openly. In this season, I learned that vulnerability requires wisdom. Not every truth needs a public audience. Not every struggle needs immediate expression. Some things must be processed privately with Christ before they can be shared safely with others. Learning when to speak and when to remain silent protected both my heart and the people connected to the assignment. Discernment became a form of care.

Responsibility also deepened my understanding of patience. I had to learn patience not only with circumstances but also with myself. Growth was not linear. Some lessons took longer than I expected. Some weaknesses required repeated correction. I had to accept that transformation does not happen on demand. It unfolds through repetition and reflection. Impatience with the process only created unnecessary tension. Patience allowed growth to take root rather than remain superficial.

Each season builds on the previous one. Nothing stands alone. The endurance developed earlier supported later responsibility. The humility learned in isolation protected me in visibility. The discipline formed in struggle prepared me for expansion. This realization gave meaning to experiences that once felt disconnected. The journey began to make sense not because answers appeared, but because patterns emerged.

What I understand now is that the battle behind the call is not meant to end quickly. It evolves. Each new level of responsibility introduces a different kind of pressure, not to punish, but to prepare. The goal is not to remove weight, but to increase capacity. Christ was not testing how much I could endure; He was teaching me how to carry what would one day be required of me without losing clarity, integrity, or peace.

CHAPTER 12

BUILDING WHAT GOD PROMISED

Building the vision Christ placed in my spirit demanded more than passion or inspiration. Sacrifice became the currency required to move forward. When Christ gives a calling larger than your resources, strength, or understanding, growth becomes the only path. It is easy to speak about faith when nothing is being asked of you, but real faith begins when stepping forward feels risky and uncomfortable, when certainty disappears and trust becomes the only foundation beneath your feet. That is where the vision for the clinic began: not in confidence, security, or abundance, but through pain, desperation, and the burden of seeing suffering transformed into hope.

The vision felt clear in my spirit, yet the process ahead felt overwhelming. Every attempt to move forward seemed to expose how unprepared I was. Fear insisted that I was reaching too far. Doubt whispered that failure would be public. Discouragement tried to convince me that I could not carry something so large. Yet the weight inside my spirit refused to let me rest. Each morning the calling pressed against my chest, reminding me that silence would be disobedience. The question was not whether the vision was real. The question was whether I was willing to sacrifice comfort to pursue what Christ called me to build.

Obedience demanded a price. Purpose required release. Every step forward costs something. Time used for rest became time spent studying, strategizing, and preparing. Financial resources meant for comfort became resources dedicated to laying a foundation for something unseen. Every decision asked me to choose calling over convenience. People could not understand why I was investing in something that had not yet materialized. They could not see what I saw. They did not feel the fire in my chest or the urgency rising in my spirit. People cannot support what they cannot see, and God often hides the fullness of a vision until obedience has already begun.

Carrying the vision alone made the journey heavier than I expected. Some relationships shifted, not because of conflict, but because growth requires separation. When Christ begins moving a person into purpose, He does not announce it to everyone. Conversations change. Access closes. People who once supported you drift away quietly. At first, the silence felt like rejection. Later, I realized Christ was protecting the assignment. Purpose is rarely built in crowds. It grows in hidden places, where there is no applause to depend on and no audience to impress.

Warfare intensified with each step forward. Opposition surfaced in unexpected forms. Illness pressed hard against my body. Dizziness struck without warning, forcing me to steady myself on walls or chairs just to remain upright. Migraines pulsed behind my eyes. Heart complications stole breath and strength. Pain made ordinary tasks feel impossible, yet teaching and ministry continued. Many nights, I finished speaking and collapsed afterward, shaking with exhaustion. Completing sessions sometimes required every ounce of strength I had left. Yet somehow, I always made it through, not by physical ability, but by grace that refused to let me fall.

Serving others while suffering personally reshaped my understanding of compassion. It revealed how deeply people hurt in silence. When continuing felt impossible, Christ reminded me of the lives connected to this vision. Families waiting for care they could not access. Children whose futures depended on medical intervention. Men and women suffering without hope. Their faces became the reason quitting was not an option. Obedience became responsibility. Purpose demanded endurance. Sacrifice became the offering.

No outside support existed during those early years. No financial assistance arrived. No promises turned into action. Progress continued only because I was willing to invest what I had. Every step toward the vision was funded personally through hard work, private sacrifice, and years of determination. Nothing had been purchased. Nothing had been built physically. Yet progress was taking place behind the scenes, brick by brick, through planning, research, and preparation. I used what was in my hands and trusted Christ for what I did not have. Faith is not waiting for resources. Faith begins with movement.

The land secured for the clinic became a physical reminder that Christ had already started what once felt impossible. While the permanent building has not yet been constructed, the mobile clinic operating in Haiti stands as evidence that the vision is alive. Those early efforts may have appeared small to the world, but they were monumental to my spirit. Faith often begins like a seed pushing through soil, unseen and unnoticed. Nothing dramatic happened overnight, yet steady progress continued, one faithful step at a time.

One scripture became an anchor when the weight felt overwhelming. Psalm 127:1 declares, "Unless the Lord builds the house, the builders labor in vain." Those words lifted pressure from my shoulders. The clinic is not dependent on my strength. Christ is the architect. My responsibility is obedience. The outcome belongs to Him.

Preparation became a way of life. Planning filled long nights. Research into legal requirements, licensing, medical compliance, nonprofit structure, and financial pathways expanded my understanding of what would be required. Progress moved slowly but intentionally. Conversations with doctors, nurses, leaders, and professionals began to provide clarity. Unexpected people appeared with insight at the exact moment discouragement tried to take hold. None of those connections happened by coincidence.

Storms continued throughout the journey. Symptoms still come without warning. Some days are heavy and overwhelming. Yet ministry does not pause when pain arrives. People continue reaching out for prayer, guidance, and support. I learned how to serve while broken, not because suffering was desirable, but because grace carried me when strength failed. Purpose became more than preaching. It became advocacy. It became intercession. It became action.

The mission is still unfolding. It is far from complete, but the foundation is real and the direction is clear. Plans are taking shape. Strategy is expanding into responsibility. Momentum is rising slowly but deliberately. A dream once held privately is becoming visible. Something sacred is being built step by step, not through comfort, but through persistence and sacrifice.

Progress does not announce itself. It unfolds gradually, built through hidden seasons of endurance, prayer, preparation, and silence. Growth demands discipline, patience, and courage. It requires releasing excuses and moving forward even when fear is loud. Leadership requires maturity beyond emotion. Purpose requires consistency beyond enthusiasm. Nothing about this process has been easy, but everything about it has been necessary.

Movement separates desire from destiny. Anyone can desire growth, but responsibility belongs to the obedient. Purpose belongs to those who do not quit. Every setback developed endurance. Every disappointment sharpened direction. Every closed door refined vision. Every test strengthened character. What once felt crushing now carries meaning. Pain became strength. Fear became focus. Calling became assignment.

Hope grows stronger with every step. Lives are waiting. Healing is possible. Transformation is near. Christ is building something too significant to rush. The foundation stands. The vision is alive. The journey continues. A new season is unfolding. Nothing ahead feels incidental. Everything carries intention. Christ is still constructing what He began, and every sign points forward. The assignment remains active. Movement has begun. The promised future is becoming reality, one step at a time.

Life no longer felt casual. Each step carried intention. Each thought connected back to purpose. Even when nothing changed outwardly, something undeniable shifted internally. A steady urgency settled beneath the surface, pushing me to keep building, planning, and preparing for what I sensed was coming. Waiting no longer felt passive. It became active participation.

Excitement and fear existed side by side. Part of me felt ready to step into what God had promised. Another part wrestled with the fear of failing publicly. Building something that had never existed before carried weight. There were nights when I sat alone, reviewing pages of notes and plans, questioning whether I could carry something so demanding. Feelings of inadequacy surfaced. Questions remained unanswered. Pressure settled heavily, and responsibility felt overwhelming. In those quiet moments, I faced what obedience truly requires.

Purpose sounds inspiring when spoken, but execution exposes insecurity, limitation, and fear. I found myself wrestling less with the vision and more with my own capacity to carry it. Could I truly build what God entrusted to me? Could I sustain a mission that impacts others beyond myself? Could I remain steady under pressure that did not ease? My doubt was never about God. It was about myself.

What began to surface was a deeper understanding that building what God promises requires accountability beyond vision alone. The clinic could not be sustained by belief without structure, nor by passion without order. I learned that responsibility often increases before results appear, and leadership is tested long before authority becomes visible.

Every decision carried implications beyond progress. It affected trust. How resources were handled, how plans were documented, and how integrity was protected in unseen moments would determine whether this vision could withstand pressure. God was teaching me that calling is proven not only through sacrifice, but through stewardship. Stewardship was revealed in how carefully I prepared for people I had not yet met.

Patience became a demanding teacher. God did not reveal the full plan, only the next step. Trusting Him one step at a time required a level of surrender I had never experienced. My spirit understood what my flesh resisted accepting: the timing was not mine to control. Each attempt to force progress led to frustration. Every time I tried to move ahead prematurely, God slowed the pace. I learned that obedience is not simply doing what God says. It is doing it when He says, how He says, and where He says, even when it does not make sense.

I spent many nights in quiet reflection, asking questions most people avoid. Why do you want this? What are you willing to sacrifice? Are you prepared to carry the weight of what you are praying for? Can you handle pressure without compromising integrity? Can you walk alone without resenting God? Those questions exposed motives and refined intention. Purpose carries weight, and God does not place responsibility on a foundation unable to support it.

While others slept, I stayed awake studying laws, policies, and medical guidelines, revising strategies and refining action steps. Hours disappeared into research. Pages of notes filled binder after binder. Documents covered the table like plans waiting to be built. Progress did not come through inspiration. It came through sacrifice. It came through persistence when exhaustion demanded rest. It came through showing up on days when strength felt absent.

The deeper I moved into preparation, the more I recognized how much God was shaping spiritual maturity behind the scenes. Prayer became deeper. Worship grew quieter but more sincere. Silence became instruction. Instead of asking God to remove challenges, I asked Him to shape my character through them. Instead of praying for strength, I prayed to be trustworthy with the strength He was giving. Instead of seeking confirmation from people, I learned to recognize peace as direction.

They did not see buildings, equipment, or funding, but they heard the seriousness in my voice and noticed the determination in my posture. They sensed something shifting, something growing beyond conversation and ideas. Purpose often reveals itself before results appear. Faith became a lifestyle rather than a concept. It meant showing up daily with discipline. It meant making decisions aligned with the future rather than the present. It required sacrificing comfort to build capacity. It required believing that what was unseen was still real. Faith became action, not inspiration.

Pressure increased as responsibility expanded. Leadership required strength beyond emotion. Vision required focus beyond distraction. Purpose required consistency beyond motivation. I began to understand that growth is not formed in moments of celebration, but cultivated during seasons of sacrifice.

One truth reshaped everything. God was not preparing a project. He was preparing a man.

The clinic was never the first assignment. Internal transformation came first. God builds leaders before He builds platforms. He shapes character before releasing responsibility. People often asked when the clinic would open, unaware that construction begins in the spirit long before it appears in the natural. God was developing patience, endurance, emotional stability, and spiritual clarity. He was increasing the capacity to carry pressure without breaking. What God builds does not collapse. What is formed in silence becomes stable.

As months turned into years, fear gave way to confidence. Not confidence in my ability, but confidence in God's. Anxiety was replaced with trust. Confusion gave way to focus. Hesitation gave way to purpose. Waiting turned into movement. Forward motion required courage. Courage meant stepping into what God called me to do even when outcomes were uncertain. It meant standing firm when my knees shook and continuing when progress moved slowly. It meant preparing diligently while trusting fully that the outcome belonged to God.

I could feel destiny drawing closer. Not loudly. Not dramatically. Quietly. Strongly. Unshakably.

Something shifted inside me from hoping the vision would happen to knowing it would. The dream no longer felt like a possibility. It became a responsibility. I stopped praying for confirmation and began praying for strategy and strength. I no longer questioned readiness. I recognized that readiness was already forming within me.

God had prepared me for the next stage, and whether anyone understood it or not, I knew deep within my spirit that a door was opening. A turning point was approaching. The future was already unfolding. The next step was waiting. Progress required more than planning and determination.

It demanded courage beyond anything I had known before. Each step required deeper sacrifice, and every decision carried weight that altered the direction of life itself. Moving forward meant leaving what was familiar, choosing action when stillness felt safer, and continuing to build while battling pain that refused to fade.

Momentum increased as the vision took shape. Actions replaced ideas. Systems replaced conversation. Strategy replaced uncertainty. Days filled with planning and long nights spent writing proposals and restructuring financial priorities began shaping reality. The process was uncomfortable, but comfort was no longer the goal. Purpose required focus, not convenience. Dreams do not grow in ease. They grow under pressure, through sacrifice and discipline.

Focus sharpened with each passing week. Tasks once delayed became urgent. Goals that once felt distant became immediate responsibility. Every step reinforced the awareness that something unprecedented was forming. Failure was not an option. Too many lives were waiting on the other side of completion. Each time my body tried to slow me with dizziness or fatigue, determination rose stronger. Nothing would stop what God had already set into motion.

Elements surrounding the vision began aligning beyond human timing. Unexpected phone calls opened conversations that once felt unreachable. Meetings that had seemed impossible were scheduled. People who did not fully understand the mission spoke about the work as if they could already see it. Professionals who once observed quietly began offering support. Each encounter confirmed that the future was closer than it appeared.

Pressure increased simultaneously. The weight of responsibility grew heavier. Decisions had to be made quickly and carefully. Each choice shaped the next stage. Every hour required intentional focus. The pace accelerated. Battles intensified. Challenges arrived without warning. Yet strength continued to rise. Something powerful had awakened, and it could no longer be silenced.

A moment arrived when hesitation was no longer an option. A decision had to be made to step fully into the future or allow the vision to stall under caution and fear. There was no middle ground. Destiny required movement. Purpose demanded action. Every sacrifice had prepared the ground for that moment. Every tear had watered seeds planted years earlier.

Silence filled the room one night as plans lay spread across the table, documents waiting for signatures, and doubt attempted to take control. Pain pulsed through my body, and exhaustion pressed heavily, yet the call within me refused to quiet. Something shifted. Something ignited. A certainty rose in my spirit that the time had arrived. There was no turning back. No hesitation. No waiting for clarity that would only come through movement.

My hands trembled slightly as I signed the papers that committed everything. That signature marked the moment when faith became action. It separated the past from the future. It represented stepping into territory that could not be reversed. Each breath felt like entering a battle with no retreat, stepping forward without a map, and committing to a future that required full surrender. Everything changed in that moment. Pressure turned into momentum. Fear turned into fuel. Uncertainty turned into direction. The atmosphere shifted. The weight that once felt overwhelming transformed into strength. The vision that once seemed impossible became undeniable.

That whisper carried an urgency that ignited a fire nothing could extinguish. It was no longer about hope or possibility. It was about inevitability. The vision had crossed a threshold, and nothing would ever be the same. Whatever lay ahead would require everything within me. The battles to come would demand the strongest version of who I had become. The next season would not be gentle. It would change everything.

When God places a calling inside a person's spirit, the vision often arrives long before the resources. That reality became clear the moment I committed to building the clinic God placed in my heart. The work required more than excitement or words. It demanded time, energy, discipline, planning, and a firm decision to keep moving even when progress felt invisible.

There were seasons when results could not be seen, yet something shifted quietly within me, reminding me that growth does not always begin publicly. It begins in silence, in unseen places where resolve is tested and foundations are formed.

Progress required financial sacrifice beyond comfort. Investing in the future meant letting go of things that once felt normal. Every decision required intention. Every dollar carried purpose. Every hour demanded discipline. While many assumed support was coming from donors or outside organizations, most progress was built through personal sacrifice. I chose to invest in the vision before asking anyone else to believe in it. Purpose required proof of commitment. It mattered that God saw my full investment in what He entrusted to me. I was not building from abundance. I was building from obedience.

The emotional weight of responsibility became as real as the financial strain. Carrying something meant to serve others can feel overwhelming when progress appears slow. There were days when exhaustion whispered that the vision was too large and the burden too heavy. In those moments, I questioned whether I had misunderstood God. I questioned whether I could build something with such impact.

The questions were heavy, and silence offered no immediate answers. Yet quitting never felt like an option. Something within me refused to release the assignment. Giving up did not feel safe. Obedience remained the only way forward.

Planning demanded more than enthusiasm. It required research, structure, and education. I spent countless nights studying healthcare laws, nonprofit requirements, financial forecasting, medical licensing procedures, and international logistics. The process felt intimidating. Many nights, I sat with documents spread across my desk, overwhelmed by how much I did not know. Each new piece of information revealed another layer of responsibility. The work was slow. The progress was uncomfortable. But growth never comes through comfort. It comes through challenge. Every step forced the kind of development leadership requires.

Discipline became the anchor. People often talk about dreams as if they manifest through emotion alone, but I learned that purpose demands consistency. I woke up early to work on plans. I stayed up late to complete necessary tasks. Weekends disappeared into writing proposals, building strategies, and communicating with professionals in the medical field. Planning replaced entertainment. Focus replaced distraction. Rest became a luxury rather than a guarantee. The cost was high, but it never felt wasted. It felt like preparation for something far larger than me.

The process exposed weaknesses that required correction. I had to confront habits that limited my capacity. Some days, it was uncomfortable to admit how much improvement was needed. There were moments of frustration when I expected progress to move faster, but God was training patience and endurance. I learned that purpose cannot be rushed. Growth cannot be microwaved. God builds slowly because He builds deeply. Anything meant to last requires time and structure.

One scripture became a steady reminder during the most overwhelming seasons of planning. Psalm 37 verse 5 (NIV) says, "Commit your way to the Lord. Trust in Him and He will do this." Those words became a quiet reassurance that the outcome did not depend solely on my strength. Whenever anxiety settled in my chest, that scripture lifted the weight. God was not asking me to build alone. He was asking me to trust Him and keep moving. That truth became the foundation that held me steady.

Building the vision brought pressure that tested the structure of my faith. Pain in my body continued unpredictably. Dizziness arrived at inconvenient moments, and migraines forced me to pause when I wanted to keep working. Physical weakness pressed against determination and reminded me that progress would not come through human strength. In the middle of that pressure, God continued to provide just enough strength for the next step. The fact that the work continued despite sickness and struggle became evidence that grace was carrying me.

The sacrifices quietly reshaped my identity. Fear began to lose control. Doubt weakened. Confidence grew, not in myself, but in what God was doing through me. The more I worked, the clearer it became that the calling was not designed for applause or recognition. It was designed for service and responsibility. The vision was not a dream to admire. It was a mission to complete. What once felt like a burden became a blessing, and every setback became another reason to rise stronger.

There were mornings when strength felt limited and every decision demanded more clarity than I believed I had. That tension forced maturity in how I approached purpose. I learned that destiny is not built on desire alone. It is shaped by structure, responsibility, and accountability.

If I wanted to build something that could stand for generations, I had to think beyond the temporary and beyond myself. I had to consider systems and sustainability. I needed to build something that would continue even if I were no longer present to guide it. This shift changed the weight of the assignment. It was no longer about proving anything to anyone. It became about the lives depending on my obedience.

Passion can start a race, but endurance finishes it. Many people are eager to begin something new, but excitement fades quickly. Leadership required commitment even when motivation disappeared. I began managing time more intentionally, organizing my days around purpose rather than convenience. I learned that progress is built in the details.

Small choices determine the direction of large dreams. The clinic required planning that stretched my thinking far beyond comfort. It demanded education, study, and countless hours researching financial systems, medical needs, and legal processes. Some nights did not end until sunrise. Some days required pushing through pain without excuse. Growth no longer allowed emotion to lead. It required discipline instead.

As responsibilities grew heavier, fear and insecurity tried to rise again, because stepping into unknown territory forces you to confront everything you once believed about yourself. There were moments when I questioned whether I was qualified to build something so significant.

Doubt whispered that someone else could do it better, faster, or easier. Confidence did not always come naturally. It had to be developed, strengthened intentionally through prayer, reflection, and persistent movement. I discovered that faith is not a feeling. Faith is continuing when feeling disappears.

Every step revealed that the vision was bigger than I had imagined. I could feel God shaping a capacity inside me that I did not know existed. The man who once struggled simply to survive now stood in a place where survival was no longer enough. I was being stretched to grow into leadership that demanded endurance, wisdom, and a deeper reliance on Christ. Everything about the process reminded me that the clinic was not just a project. It was part of a divine assignment, being built day by day through obedience. The weight of that truth humbled me. I understood that the responsibility I carried was sacred.

As the future began to unfold, it became clear that nothing about this journey would be ordinary. Nothing would be accidental. Every step required intention and trust. Revelation settled into my spirit: the clinic would not only heal bodies, it would restore dignity, hope, and faith. People who once felt forgotten would discover that Christ had not abandoned them. Families who believed they were out of options would find new possibilities. Children denied care would receive treatment without fear of cost. The vision was never about concrete walls; it was about living vessels carrying the love of Christ to broken places.

Jeremiah 29:11 (NIV) echoed powerfully within me during those months of building and planning: "For I know the plans I have for you," declares the Lord, "plans to prosper you and not to harm you, plans to give you hope and a future." Those words were not merely motivating, they were instructions. They reminded me that every battle, setback, and sacrifice was part of a plan far greater than I could see. I held onto those words tightly, especially in the moments when progress felt slow and answers seemed buried beneath uncertainty.

Jean Joseph

CHAPTER 13

THOSE WHO LIFTED ME WHEN I COULD NOT STAND

Strength is often misrepresented as independence, but my life has shown that endurance is rarely sustained alone. Purpose does not unfold in isolation, no matter how personal the calling may feel. Every assignment God places in a life is accompanied by people He appoints to steady the journey when internal strength begins to fail.

I learned this not in theory, but through seasons when my body weakened, my clarity blurred, and my ability to continue depended heavily on the presence of others who refused to step away. I am standing today not because I was strong enough on my own, but because people remained close during moments when standing required more than I could produce.

My wife has been central to that steadiness in ways words can barely capture. She witnessed every physical battle, every health crisis, and every moment when quitting felt more reasonable than continuing. When vertigo left me disoriented and unstable, she was present without panic. When words failed and confidence thinned, she prayed without hesitation.

There were nights when my body resisted movement and my mind wrestled with uncertainty, yet she stood beside me with a calm resolve that anchored the space around us. Her presence was not reactive or emotional. It was consistent, measured, and unwavering, allowing me to breathe through moments that could have easily broken my resolve.

As responsibility increased and ministry placed heavier demands on our home, she did not resist the cost. She absorbed weight quietly and adjusted without complaint. The sacrifices required were not always visible and rarely acknowledged publicly, yet they shaped the stability that allowed purpose to continue moving forward.

She honored the call on my life even when it required personal restraint, delayed comfort, and emotional endurance. Her faith did not fluctuate with circumstances. It remained steady, creating a foundation that fear could not dismantle. When everything else felt unstable, her consistency grounded me.

Another steady presence throughout this journey has been my mother-in-law, whose compassion is expressed through action rather than words. Long before there was anything tangible to show for the vision, she believed in it. She gave generously to care for children without seeking recognition or validation.

Her commitment helped sustain the twenty-four children connected to this mission and strengthened the foundation of the work in ways that may never be fully measured. Her faithfulness was neither seasonal nor conditional. It was consistent, quiet, and deeply rooted in conviction rather than visibility. She demonstrated love not through explanation, but through reliability.

Family also played an essential role during seasons when emotional and mental pressure became heavy. My brothers and sisters remained present even when the vision was difficult to explain and the process lacked clarity.

They listened when my thoughts felt scattered and offered grounding perspective when confusion clouded direction. Their willingness to remain close without requiring full understanding reinforced a lesson I learned repeatedly: commitment does not demand complete comprehension. It requires presence, patience, and trust.

My thoughts often return to my mother and the example of endurance she modeled long before I understood the true meaning of resilience. Her sacrifices formed the backbone of the perseverance that later carried me through my hardest seasons.

I remember watching her leave early and return late, working tirelessly to create a future that required personal sacrifice. She did not complain, and she did not allow hardship to strip her dignity. Her strength was quiet, steady, and unshakable. That example shaped my understanding of responsibility long before my calling ever became clear.

One moment remains vivid and defining. After I stopped attending school and was removed from enrollment, shame consumed me. When the school contacted her, she did not raise her voice or humiliate me. She sat quietly as tears fell, and that silence reached deeper than any punishment could have. The following morning, before sunrise, she spoke words that altered the direction of my life. She told me quitting was not an option and that God did not bring me into this world to disappear. Those words planted seeds of purpose long before I understood their meaning.

Throughout the journey, many individuals crossed my path at moments when their presence mattered more than they likely realized. Some were friends who walked closely for a season; others were strangers who offered timely encouragement or assistance.

Some contributed financially for a short time, while others prayed quietly without recognition. Even when certain relationships ended before results became visible, their impact remained significant. Influence is not measured by how long someone stays; it is measured by how deeply their presence shapes the direction of your life.

The twenty-four children connected to this mission reshaped my understanding of responsibility in ways that cannot be summarized quickly. Their lives gave weight to the vision when exhaustion pressed hard and progress felt slow. Each child carried a story that deepened resolve and clarified purpose. Serving them revealed that ministry is not built on recognition, comfort, or momentum. It is built through consistent care, responsibility, and the willingness to continue showing up when strength feels limited.

I remember watching a young boy stand at the end of a food line holding a small container. His clothes were worn, and his shoes barely held together, yet gratitude filled his face when he received his portion. Later, I learned that he intentionally saved half each time for a younger sibling who could not make the walk. That moment revealed generosity in its purest form and reshaped my understanding of sacrifice more powerfully than any sermon ever could.

On another day, a young girl arrived with tears in her eyes, unable to lift her head. She whispered that she had lost her mother and felt invisible in a world that had become too heavy for her age. She prayed each night for someone who cared. Holding her as she cried permanently altered my understanding of ministry. The mission was never about food alone. It was about restoring dignity, hope, and faith to hearts that felt forgotten.

Scripture reflects this reality clearly. Ecclesiastes 4:9–10 reminds us that two are better than one, not because effort is reduced, but because endurance increases. I fell many times throughout this journey. I was lifted many times as well. I did not rise alone, and I was never meant to.

Leadership often becomes isolating as responsibility grows. Decisions carry weight, mistakes affect others, and clarity is not always shared. During those seasons, having people who could listen without judgment preserved emotional balance. They did not rush to fix problems or force solutions.

Their presence created space for honesty, reflection, and recovery, which proved essential for long-term endurance.

What sustained this journey most was not loud support or constant reassurance, but the steady presence of people who acted without needing acknowledgment. Responsibility was carried quietly, details were handled without announcement, and pressure was reduced before it had time to overwhelm. That kind of care revealed maturity, not obligation. It demonstrated ownership of the mission rather than temporary involvement, and it preserved momentum during seasons when explanation would have cost more energy than I could give.

Pressure to keep moving forward often collided with physical limitation, emotional fatigue, and responsibilities that refused to slow down. During those seasons, the people closest to me recognized warning signs before I was willing to acknowledge them. They noticed when my pace became unsustainable and when determination quietly turned into depletion. Their awareness protected me from collapsing under expectations I would have carried without question. That kind of attentiveness does not come from obligation. It grows from genuine care built over time.

Ongoing health challenges added an unpredictable layer to every decision. Dizziness, migraines, and physical instability disrupted plans without warning and reshaped what productivity looked like daily. Energy could disappear suddenly, leaving unfinished responsibilities and unanswered questions behind. The people around me adapted without frustration or resentment. They learned how to step in without overstepping and how to give space without withdrawing. Their flexibility preserved dignity and progress at the same time, allowing the journey to continue even when my body resisted it.

Extended periods of silence became necessary, not because trust was broken, but because explanation required more energy than I had available.

Carrying responsibility while managing physical weakness often left little room for conversation. Those who understood that silence was sometimes part of survival offered a rare kind of strength. They did not demand clarity or emotional performance. They respected boundaries without creating distance. That respect created space for recovery and reflection without guilt, which became essential for sustainability.

Much of the care that sustained this journey arrived before I even recognized the need for it. Responsibilities were handled quietly. Details were managed without announcement. Tasks were completed without being framed as favors. These actions reduced pressure before it had time to accumulate. Care expressed through action carried more weight than reassurance ever could. It demonstrated awareness, responsibility, and shared ownership of the work, reinforcing stability during unpredictable seasons.

Steadiness proved just as important as physical assistance. Being reminded that limitation did not diminish worth preserved clarity when fatigue threatened identity. Encouragement did not always come through affirmation. At times, it came through permission to rest without apology. At other moments, it arrived as reminders that slowing down did not equal disobedience. These interventions protected perspective when exhaustion attempted to distort reality and replace discernment with guilt.

Some individuals cared enough to challenge decisions when fear began influencing judgment. They asked difficult questions without accusation and refused to allow discouragement to quietly take control. Their honesty did not undermine resolve. It strengthened it. Guidance rooted only in affirmation can weaken judgment over time, but guidance anchored in truth preserves clarity. Their willingness to speak when silence would have been easier prevented emotional reactions from overriding wisdom.

Patterns began to emerge, revealing how intentionally God placed people at different stages of the journey. Some appeared briefly but arrived at precisely the right moment. Others remained through extended seasons of uncertainty, slow progress, and repeated obstacles. Each role mattered. Length of time did not determine significance. Timing did. God positioned people exactly where stability was needed when pressure increased.

Encouragement also surfaced from unexpected places. Messages arrived from individuals who shared how something I had spoken or taught helped them endure their own season of difficulty. These words often came on days when progress felt invisible and effort went unnoticed. Hearing that the work reached farther than I could see provided confirmation without pressure and reinforced the reality that impact is not always immediate or measurable.

Working alongside others created bonds that conversation alone could never produce. Shared responsibility built trust quickly. Preparing resources, coordinating logistics, and managing details together formed connections rooted in commitment rather than convenience. These experiences transformed individual effort into collective responsibility and reinforced the understanding that purpose is strengthened when carried together.

Accepting help required humility that did not come naturally. Independence had quietly evolved into isolation, convincing me that strength meant self-reliance. Allowing others to walk closely did not weaken resolve. It preserved it. Strength expanded when it was shared rather than guarded, and endurance increased when pride loosened its hold.

Balance was sustained by people who recognized when demands exceeded capacity. They noticed when rest was necessary and when pace required adjustment. Without those interventions, exhaustion could have easily disguised itself as faithfulness. Wisdom often arrived through voices willing to act rather than remain silent, protecting longevity and preventing short-term effort from undermining long-term purpose.

Trust deepened through shared endurance rather than explanation. Words became unnecessary because presence had already communicated commitment. Standing near someone during hardship reveals character faster than conversation ever could. The people who remained steady during uncertainty demonstrated that loyalty is often quiet and unannounced. It does not demand acknowledgment. It simply stays.

Daily life continued even as responsibility expanded, and that continuity mattered. Ordinary conversations, shared routines, and moments of laughter grounded perspective when pressure threatened to distort reality. Stability often came from simple interactions that reminded me that life does not pause simply because calling intensifies.

Health limitations reshaped how relationships were navigated. Repeated explanations became exhausting, and the people who learned through observation rather than instruction preserved energy. They adapted naturally, responding to what they saw rather than what they were told. That awareness allowed function without constant justification, preserving both dignity and strength.

Certain individuals consistently reinforced the truth that worth does not decrease when productivity slows. That understanding protected me from internalizing guilt during seasons when capacity was limited. Identity remained intact even when output changed, preventing exhaustion from eroding confidence or purpose.

It became clear that some relationships were designed for specific seasons. Their absence later did not indicate failure or betrayal. It indicated transition. Releasing those connections with gratitude instead of resentment preserved peace and created space for new relationships to form naturally.

Perspective matured regarding expectations. Not everyone expresses care in the same way. Some demonstrate it through action, others through consistency. Some show up through quiet presence rather than conversation.

Recognizing these differences replaced assumption with appreciation and prevented unnecessary disappointment.

Experience reshaped how I now approach others carrying heavy responsibility. Listening replaced advice. Presence replaced urgency. Space replaced pressure. These changes did not come from strategy, they were formed through lived experience and reshaped how leadership was practiced.

As responsibility continued to expand, I became increasingly aware that endurance is not sustained by intensity, but by consistency reinforced through relationship. Motivation rises and falls, but steadiness requires something deeper than personal drive. The people who remained connected to this journey understood that calling is carried over time, not conquered in moments. They did not push for visible progress or constant updates. Instead, they valued faithfulness that remained unseen. Their approach reinforced patience and protected the work from becoming driven by pressure rather than purpose.

The longer the journey continued, the clearer it became that leadership does not simply reveal vision, it reveals dependency patterns. I had to confront areas where I leaned too heavily on certain people for reassurance and areas where I resisted help out of misplaced responsibility. Healthy interdependence developed slowly, through discomfort and correction. Balance did not arrive instantly. It was shaped through trial, reflection, and humility. Learning how to receive without surrendering direction became an essential part of maturity.

Emotional capacity requires just as much stewardship as physical energy. Carrying responsibility while managing uncertainty placed strain on internal reserves that were not immediately visible. The people closest to me recognized when emotional fatigue began influencing judgment and decision making. They did not criticize or withdraw. They offered perspective grounded in care rather than reaction. Their steadiness helped separate temporary exhaustion from permanent conclusions, preventing discouragement from reshaping direction.

Time also revealed how easily isolation can disguise itself as discipline. The belief that carrying everything alone demonstrated strength nearly undermined sustainability. Allowing others to remain close did not dilute focus. It clarified it. Shared responsibility did not weaken resolve, it reinforced it. Strength multiplied when trust replaced self-reliance and when connection replaced quiet withdrawal.

As the mission progressed, the nature of relationships shifted as well. Some individuals who once played active roles transitioned into quieter positions of encouragement. Others stepped forward with greater involvement as needs changed. Accepting these transitions without resistance preserved peace. Not every relationship is meant to remain static. Growth requires movement, and movement often reshapes proximity. Understanding this prevented resentment and allowed gratitude to remain intact even as roles evolved.

Over time, I began to understand how deeply care must be rooted in discernment. Not every burden should be shared widely. Not every struggle requires explanation. The people who honored discretion strengthened stability. They understood that protecting clarity sometimes required privacy. That respect safeguarded both the mission and the relationships connected to it.

Experience also sharpened my awareness of how quickly exhaustion can distort perception. When capacity is depleted, everything feels heavier and more urgent than it truly is. The people who assisted with slow, deliberate decision-making during those moments preserved wisdom. Their patience prevented reactive choices driven by fatigue rather than discernment. That restraint protected long-term vision from short-term strain.

Over time, gratitude required intentional focus. Pressure naturally draws attention toward what remains undone. Pausing to recognize those who carried weight alongside me protected humility and prevented frustration from shaping leadership. Gratitude became a discipline rather than an emotion. It grounded perspective and reinforced the truth that nothing meaningful is built alone.

The presence of others also reshaped how success was defined. Progress was no longer measured by speed or visibility; it was measured by sustainability. The people who remained near reinforced that endurance mattered more than expansion and that faithfulness mattered more than recognition. Their influence helped guard the mission from being driven by urgency instead of obedience.

Shared belief in the assignment created alignment that transcended differences in personality and perspective. Agreement did not require uniform thinking; it required mutual respect and shared values. That alignment allowed collaboration to function without unnecessary conflict and enabled disagreement without division. Unity was built through trust rather than control.

The children connected to this work continued to shape decisions even from a distance. Their growth reinforced responsibility. Their needs sharpened focus. Their resilience reminded me why consistency mattered even when energy was limited. Knowing that lives depended on steady commitment strengthened resolve during seasons when personal motivation fluctuated.

Encounters with families affected by the mission clarified priorities beyond theory. Hearing stories firsthand transformed abstract vision into tangible responsibility. These experiences deepened commitment and reinforced the importance of remaining grounded in compassion rather than ambition. Purpose became less about building something impressive and more about remaining faithful to the people placed directly in our care.

As reflection deepened, it became evident that many pivotal moments could have unfolded differently without people stepping in quietly at just the right time. Decisions influenced by encouragement, restraint offered during fatigue, and reminders delivered at critical moments shaped outcomes more than visible milestones ever could. What appeared ordinary in the moment later revealed itself as essential.

Receiving care also reshaped how I extend it to others. Awareness increased. Sensitivity sharpened. Patience expanded. Experience taught me how to remain present without attempting to fix, how to listen without rushing to respond, and how to offer steadiness without creating dependence. Leadership matured through observation as much as instruction.

Over time, trust became rooted in shared history rather than constant reassurance. Familiarity created understanding without explanation. That shared history provided peace during uncertainty and stability during transition. Relationships built this way did not require performance to remain intact. They endured because they were rooted in commitment rather than convenience.

Looking ahead, clarity remains firm. God never designs calling to be endured in isolation. He weaves people into the process intentionally, each contributing in ways that sustain endurance and protect integrity. The journey has made it clear that resilience is not self-generated. It is formed through humility, connection, and shared responsibility carried over time.

CHAPTER 14

THE MIRACLE OF LIFE

Life does not always announce what it is about to do. Some seasons arrive quietly and still change everything. A person can wake up thinking they are walking into an ordinary day, only to discover later that the day carried a turning point. We often expect God to move through dramatic moments that everyone can see, but many of His greatest works happen where no one is watching.

Real transformation usually begins in the unseen places, inside the heart and mind, where pressure builds and faith is tested. The miracle of life is not only that we experience change, but that we survive what should have broken us, and we become different because of it.

What people call victory is not always loud or obvious. Sometimes victory looks like waking up after a night of battle and still choosing to stand. It looks like returning to daily responsibilities when your emotions are tired and your body wants to quit. It looks like taking one more step when motivation is gone and hope feels thin. Many people walk through storms privately, carrying burdens that never show on their faces.

Yet they keep moving. They keep functioning. They keep pressing forward. When you look back and realize you lived through what once felt impossible, you begin to understand that endurance is more than personality. Endurance is often the evidence that God was active long before His hand became visible.

Some of the deepest wars are not fought in public. They are fought in the mind. Fear, anxiety, regret, responsibility, and unanswered questions can collide inside a person until rest feels impossible. I lived in that place for years. When my head touched the pillow, my thoughts did not slow down. They multiplied. Every responsibility replayed itself.

Every fear argued for control. Every concern tried to become a crisis. I learned how to function while drained and appear steady while collapsing internally. I accepted it as normal because it lasted so long that I began to believe it would never change.

Then God interrupted that reality in a way I still struggle to explain. In a dream that felt more real than anything I had ever experienced, Christ spoke to me with a clarity that cut through years of noise. He told me to stop thinking, and I responded honestly that I did not know how.

The response was simple and direct. "I am going to help you."

When I woke up, nothing looked different. Life continued. Days passed. There was no public sign, no moment to announce, no dramatic event that anyone would recognize as supernatural.

Yet one day, sitting in my living room, I noticed something that felt impossible. The racing thoughts were gone. Peace replaced pressure. Rest came without effort. The storm did not slowly fade. It disappeared so quietly that I could not even identify the exact moment it left, but I knew it was gone.

That experience reshaped the way I understand divine intervention. God does not always heal in ways that impress people. Sometimes He heals in ways that rebuild the person. He restores quietly so the transformation becomes deep. He moves in hidden places so identity can be strengthened from the inside out.

Psalm 4:8 (NIV) became real to me, not as a quote, but as a lived reality: "In peace I will lie down and sleep, for you alone, Lord, make me dwell in safety." I had read verses like that for years, but reading them and living them are not the same thing. The peace that arrived was not created by effort. It was given. That peace became proof that God can step into the most private part of a person's life and restore what no human strategy can repair.

Once you experience something like that, you stop measuring God's work by spectacle. You start paying attention to what has changed inside you. You notice how often God works without noise. You realize that many breakthroughs are recognized only in reflection, after the heart has already been reshaped. That is why some of the strongest believers are not the ones with the loudest stories, but the ones who learned how to stand while trembling, pray while hurting, and hope while waiting. Internal transformation creates a steadiness that cannot be manufactured, because it was formed under pressure.

When you look back over what you have survived, a pattern begins to emerge. You remember seasons that felt unbearable, delays that tested patience, and questions that never received immediate answers. At the time, it may have felt like silence, but reflection reveals something else. God was present even when He seemed quiet.

He was strengthening, guiding, and rebuilding without announcing Himself. Survival becomes more than endurance. It becomes evidence. Faith stops being an idea and becomes confidence, because you realize that what should have consumed you did not win.

The miracle of life is not limited to rare events. It reveals itself in ordinary moments that carry spiritual weight. Peace returning after chaos is a miracle. Hope rising after disappointment is a miracle. A person still standing after a season that tried to crush them is a miracle.

God does not intervene only to provide relief. He intervenes to prepare people for assignments. What He restores internally becomes the foundation for what He builds externally. That is why nothing is wasted. Every storm strengthens something. Every delay teaches something. Even the seasons that felt empty were doing work beneath the surface.

Relationships also become one of the clearest ways God reveals His involvement. Many blessings do not fall from the sky. They walk into our lives as people, sometimes ordinary in appearance but powerful in purpose. Some remain for years and shape us through patience, wisdom, and accountability. Others arrive for a season, teach what must be learned, and then step away when that part of the journey is complete.

God uses connection to strengthen what we could not strengthen alone, to confirm what we were too tired to believe, and to steady us when pressure begins to shake the foundation. When you look closely, you realize that certain encounters were not accidental. They were positioned.

Proverbs 11:25 (NIV) speaks to this principle clearly: "A generous person will prosper; whoever refreshes others will be refreshed." Generosity is not limited to money. It is presence. It is time. It is encouragement that arrives at the right moment. It is a conversation that prevents collapse. It is a prayer spoken in private that strengthens someone who never knew it was happening. When kindness arrives exactly when it is needed, it becomes difficult to call it coincidence. It looks like God moving through human hands, turning simple acts into protection.

As life progresses, gratitude deepens for those who remained consistent when others drifted away. Often, the strongest help came through gestures that did not draw attention. A message that arrived at the right time. A check-in that reminded me I was not alone. A person who listened without trying to fix everything. These moments did not remove the weight of life, but they strengthened me enough to carry it. God often builds endurance through the faithfulness of people who stay close and steady.

Scripture also offers a clear picture of quiet suffering turning into sudden transformation. The woman with the issue of blood carried pain for twelve years. Her condition affected her health, her finances, her dignity, and her connection to community. She searched for help and found none. As time passed, her situation grew more hopeless. Yet when she heard that Jesus was near, something inside her refused to quit. She did not have strength, status, or certainty. She had faith, and faith moved her forward.

She pressed through the crowd, not because she felt powerful, but because she believed something could change if she reached for Him. Her breakthrough came in a moment that required no stage or attention. Mark 5:29 (NIV) says, "Immediately her bleeding stopped and she felt in her body that she was freed from her suffering." That is how God works at times. A story that took years to endure can shift in a single moment when His power touches it. Her healing restored more than her body. It restored identity and dignity. When Jesus called her "Daughter," He was not only acknowledging her faith. He was restoring her sense of belonging.

That story carries a message for anyone living with delayed answers. It speaks to those fighting private battles while trying to remain steady and unseen. It confirms that faith is not measured by physical strength. It is measured by movement. She was weak and still reached. She was exhausted and still reached. She was alone and still reached. Her persistence became the bridge between suffering and restoration. The lesson is simple but firm. Faith is not proven when everything goes right. Faith is proven when everything goes wrong and you still reach for Christ.

Many people are waiting for God to intervene right now. Some are praying for healing that feels impossible. Others are praying for restoration where the damage seems permanent. Some smile in public while fighting battles in their minds every night. For those people, endurance is not weakness. It is warfare. Persistence is not small. It is spiritual strength. Even the decision to get up and try again can be evidence that heaven is holding them. Some days the miracle is not a sudden change in circumstances. Some days the miracle is the strength to keep going without collapsing.

Isaiah 40:31 (NIV) describes what renewal looks like when God restores a life: "But those who hope in the Lord will renew their strength. They will soar on wings like eagles. They will run and not grow weary. They will walk and not be faint." Renewal is a mark of His presence. Strength returning after exhaustion is not always human ability. Often it is divine empowerment. God does not only restore what was lost. He creates strength that did not exist before.

Breakthrough changes more than circumstances. It reshapes identity. A person begins to see themselves through God's eyes rather than through fear. The mind stops rehearsing defeat and starts expecting victory. Hope grows louder than doubt. Faith becomes more than a statement. It becomes a way of living. When that shift happens internally, darkness cannot fully silence it again, because it was formed through experience, not theory.

Every act of divine intervention carries purpose. God does not move only to provide relief. He moves to prepare His children for what comes next. What feels like waiting may be training. What feels like delay may be alignment. What feels like breaking may be rebuilding. Romans 5:3–4 (NIV) explains this process clearly: "Suffering produces perseverance; perseverance, character; and character, hope." That progression is not poetic. It is practical. Perseverance builds endurance. Character forms integrity. Hope becomes the anchor that holds a person steady when life shakes everything else.

Looking ahead feels different after God restores a life from the inside out. The future is no longer only intimidating. It becomes purposeful. Every challenge becomes another opportunity to experience God again. Every obstacle becomes a chance to witness His faithfulness in action. The past stops being a prison and becomes proof that God finishes what He starts. Confidence rises, not because of personal ability, but because God has already revealed what He can do in hidden places.

The miracle of life is that the story is still unfolding. There is more ahead than behind. Healing remains possible. Strength continues to develop. Purpose is still taking shape. The evidence lives in endurance.

When peace returned to my mind, I realized how much I had been surviving without noticing what that survival was costing. When God quieted the noise, I could finally hear what exhaustion had been masking. I could finally admit what pressure had been concealing. I did not just feel calmer. I felt awake. I felt clear. I felt able to breathe without fighting for every breath.

That clarity revealed something else. Strength can be built through stubbornness, but wholeness is built through surrender. Strength can be formed through pride, but wholeness grows through humility. Strength can come from self-reliance, but wholeness is formed through dependence on God. I began to see that God was not only rescuing me from anxiety. He was rescuing me from a way of living that kept me productive but not peaceful, active but not grounded, moving but not healed.

Once the internal battle shifted, my perspective on everyday life shifted with it. Ordinary moments began to feel like gifts. Rest became sacred. Silence stopped feeling empty and started feeling safe. Moments that once would have been rushed became moments I wanted to honor.

I stopped treating life like an emergency and started treating it like something God had entrusted to me. That change did not make everything easier, but it made everything more meaningful. It reminded me that the miracle of life is not only what God does around you. It is what God does within you, and how that inner work changes the way you move through the world.

I began to notice how many people are carrying the same invisible pressure I once carried. They smile, work, serve, and show up, but inside they are overwhelmed by thoughts they cannot quiet. They are trying to hold families together, meet responsibilities, remain faithful, and keep going while their minds never rest.

They feel guilty for being tired, ashamed for needing help, and afraid to admit how heavy life has become. Observing this deepened my compassion because I recognized the signs. I recognized the language. I recognized the look in the eyes of someone who is present in the room while fighting a private war.

That is where the miracle becomes a message. When God changes you privately, He is also preparing you to carry others wisely. Not by trying to fix everyone, but by knowing how to stand near people without judgment, how to listen without rushing, and how to speak life without pretending struggle does not exist.

It is easy to speak about hope when the mind is quiet and the body is strong. It is different after living through nights when hope felt unreachable. That kind of experience produces a tenderness that cannot be taught. It produces patience that cannot be forced. It produces discernment that recognizes pain even when it is hidden behind strength.

The longer I reflected, the more I understood that the miracle of life also includes God's timing. He rarely changes everything in the way we expect, and He rarely moves at the pace we demand. He works in layers because He is not only interested in relief. He is interested in transformation.

There were seasons when I asked God to remove certain burdens quickly, not realizing that the burden was developing something in me that comfort could not produce. Looking back, I see that some prayers were not delayed because God was absent. They were delayed because God was building capacity, and capacity takes time.

This is why seasons that feel slow often become the seasons that shape us most. They strip away false confidence. They expose weak foundations. They reveal what we rely on when nothing seems to be working. They confront motives and refine the heart. They teach faithfulness without applause. They teach obedience without immediate reward. They teach perseverance when stopping feels easier. In those seasons, God is not punishing us. He is preparing us, and preparation is often quiet, uncomfortable, and unseen.

God can step into a life that has been chaotic for a long time and change it without strain. He can remove what feels permanent without needing permission from fear. He can replace torment with calm so completely that a person wakes up one day and realizes the storm has ended. That is the God we serve. A God who does not always announce His work, but whose work becomes undeniable.

From that place, I began to view life as stewardship. Not only the mission or the ministry, but my mind, my body, my relationships, my time, and my decisions. I came to understand that my health is not only something to manage. It is something to honor. My peace is not just a feeling. It is a responsibility. My rest is not laziness. It is obedience when God calls me to slow down. When God gives peace, He is not only offering comfort. He is creating an environment where purpose can grow without being choked by anxiety.

The miracle of life is also seen in how God continues to open doors after long seasons of struggle. He does not disqualify a person because they battled internally. He does not abandon a calling because the journey was messy. He does not cancel destiny because someone needed time to heal. Instead, He rebuilds and then sends. He restores and then assigns. He strengthens and then expands. The process is personal, but the outcome reaches beyond the individual, because what God develops within you is meant to bless others through you.

The years of carrying pressure were not wasted. God used them. He used them to shape spiritual maturity. He used them to deepen compassion. He used them to develop endurance. He used them to prepare my heart to carry a vision that includes people who are suffering, people who are waiting, and people who need more than words.

When you survive what you once believed would destroy you, doubt loses its grip. You stop underestimating how quickly God can shift a story. You stop believing the lie that you are stuck forever. You learn that one encounter with Christ can rewrite years of struggle, and one moment of divine intervention can restore what you assumed was lost. You begin to live with expectation, not because life becomes perfect, but because God proves faithful.

The miracle of life is not only that we keep breathing. The miracle of life is that God keeps building. He keeps restoring. He keeps strengthening. He keeps guiding. He keeps shaping the future while we are still trying to understand the present. And when the next season arrives, it will not be built on fear, because fear has already been confronted. It will not be built on anxiety, because anxiety has already been quieted. It will be built on trust, on endurance, and on the evidence that God has already proven Himself in the hidden places.

What ultimately became clear through everything I endured is that God's involvement in my life was never dependent on my awareness of it. He was present in moments when I doubted Him, steady in seasons when my faith felt inconsistent, and active even when my prayers felt incomplete.

The strength that carried me forward was not something I discovered within myself, nor was it something I built through discipline alone. It was strength given over time, layered quietly through endurance, shaped through difficulty, and sustained through grace. Looking back, I can see that many of the moments I labeled as survival were actually preservation. God was not merely helping me endure hardship. He was protecting something He intended to use later.

Life itself began to feel different once that realization settled in. Ordinary days no longer felt insignificant. Rest carried meaning because I understood how easily it could be taken away. Peace felt sacred because I remembered what it was like to live without it. Faith matured beyond emotional response and became rooted in experience.

I stopped evaluating God's presence based on what I could immediately see or feel and began recognizing Him through the stability He created within me. My confidence no longer rose and fell with circumstances. It became anchored in the knowledge that God had already carried me through what I once believed would destroy me.

What changed most was not my environment, but my internal posture. Fear lost its ability to control decisions. Anxiety no longer dictated direction. Pressure no longer felt like an emergency demanding immediate reaction. Discernment developed. Patience strengthened. Perspective widened. I began to understand that God often prepares people internally long before He changes anything externally.

The endurance developed during silent seasons became the capacity required for responsibility that could not have been carried earlier. Had the future arrived sooner, it would have crushed me. God's timing was not delay. It was protection.

There were moments when I questioned whether anything meaningful was happening at all. Progress felt slow. Answers felt distant. Growth felt invisible. Yet beneath the surface, something was still forming. Faith was learning how to function without constant reassurance. Obedience was being refined without applause. Trust was being strengthened without explanation.

These were not lessons that could be learned through comfort. They required pressure, waiting, and surrender without clarity. Only later did it become evident that those seasons formed a foundation strong enough to support what was coming next.

Endurance reshaped how I understood purpose. I stopped viewing purpose as something dramatic or externally impressive and began recognizing it through responsibility, faithfulness, and consistency. Purpose was no longer tied to outcomes. It became tied to obedience.

Showing up mattered more than being seen. Remaining steady mattered more than moving quickly. Carrying responsibility with integrity mattered more than producing visible results. These shifts did not happen overnight. They developed gradually as experience corrected expectation and maturity replaced urgency.

Life also revealed how easily people underestimate what they have already survived. Many individuals wait for confirmation that God is with them while standing in the evidence of His faithfulness. Survival itself becomes testimony when viewed honestly.

The fact that I continued moving forward while managing fear, uncertainty, and exhaustion was not coincidence. It was grace at work long before I had language for it. God was reinforcing my capacity to endure without announcing His presence, and that quiet reinforcement changed how I now interpret hardship.

What once felt overwhelming began to feel instructive. Difficulty no longer signaled failure. It signaled development. Resistance no longer meant opposition alone. It often meant preparation. Even moments that felt like loss revealed lessons that later proved essential. The patience learned through waiting strengthened discernment. The humility learned through weakness preserved clarity. The discipline learned through limitation protected longevity. Nothing was wasted, even when it felt unbearable at the time.

This understanding altered how I approach the future. I no longer rush toward outcomes or fear delays. I trust that God is building something deeper than immediate results. I recognize that clarity often follows obedience rather than precedes it. Direction becomes clearer after movement, not before it. Strength grows through use, not avoidance. Confidence develops through experience, not prediction. These truths have grounded my faith in something steady rather than fragile.

Life continues with responsibility, uncertainty, and unanswered questions, but it also continues with assurance. I now understand that God does not abandon people in silence. He works within it. He does not withdraw during difficulty. He strengthens within it. He does not wait for perfection before moving. He moves within weakness. That understanding reshapes how challenges are faced and how decisions are made. Fear no longer carries the authority it once did.

I am not waiting for life to become easier. I am prepared for it to remain demanding. The difference now is that endurance has replaced panic, discernment has replaced reaction, and faith has replaced fear. I move forward with the awareness that God has already proven Himself faithful in ways that future uncertainty cannot undo.

This becomes stewardship. Each breath carries responsibility. Each step forward carries purpose. Each challenge carries the opportunity for growth rather than retreat. What once felt like barely surviving revealed itself as preparation for something greater. God did not simply help me endure. He shaped who I became through the process.

CHAPTER 15
THE BLUEPRINT OF FAITH

Vision changes the moment it begins to take form beyond imagination. It is one thing to carry a dream privately, tucked safely inside the heart where it is protected from criticism and untouched by responsibility. It is something entirely different when that same dream demands structure, timelines, resources, and commitment. When the vision for the clinic shifted from a hope whispered in prayer to an assignment that required planning, the weight of responsibility became real in a way I could never have anticipated. It was no longer something I simply believed in. It became something I had to build.

It required discipline, research, structure, and countless hours of study. Much of the process unfolded in quiet moments when no one was watching. I sat surrounded by notebooks, architectural outlines, medical requirement lists, equipment costs, and staffing projections. There was no applause in those hours and no visible progress to post or celebrate publicly. These were the unseen stages of purpose, where progress is measured not by excitement but by perseverance.

What I discovered quickly was that the journey from vision to reality is shaped more by patience than passion. Passion may ignite a dream in the beginning, but patience sustains it. Every plan required clarity. Every step required intentionality. I spent long nights reading state regulations, licensing procedures, and construction guidelines. I researched the equipment necessary for different levels of medical care and studied how to structure a sustainable facility from the ground up.

Those hours taught me that faith is not proven by emotion but by consistency. Progress was rarely dramatic. Some days I moved only an inch. On other days, the work felt overwhelming and slow. I learned to celebrate persistence rather than speed. Forward is forward, no matter how small the step.

The clinic has always represented more than a building. It represents dignity for families who deserve access to care without complication, humiliation, or financial fear. It represents a safe place for children who cannot afford to wait for help. It represents healing for people who have learned to suffer in silence. It reflects the belief that quality care should not be a luxury accessible only to the privileged.

That understanding fueled every stage of planning. On days when discouragement tried to settle into my spirit, purpose reminded me why quitting would cost more than continuing ever would. Hope requires construction. Purpose requires sacrifice. Vision requires labor. The dream became real when I understood that the blueprint was not only architectural but spiritual. The clinic is not simply a facility. It is a mission.

During the planning process, one scripture became a source of steady strength: Isaiah 60:22 (NIV), which declares, "When the time is right, I, the Lord, will make it happen." That promise lifted the weight off my shoulders. It reminded me that while I am responsible for obedience, God is responsible for timing.

I do not have to manipulate outcomes or rush what God is preparing. My responsibility is to build faithfully. His responsibility is to complete what He has started. Understanding this truth allowed me to work without anxiety, trusting that every hour of preparation is already connected to future fulfillment.

Leadership, I learned, carries a weight that is difficult to explain. When a calling begins to impact people beyond yourself, life changes. Decisions can no longer be made casually. Time cannot be wasted carelessly. Leadership demands sacrifice, not only of energy but of comfort. It requires the ability to carry responsibility even when no one else understands its weight.

People often see the results of leadership but rarely witness the cost. They see strength on the outside but do not see the internal stretching leadership demands. They hear confidence in a voice but do not hear the internal conversations that shaped it. They witness outcomes but know nothing of private prayers, lonely nights, or difficult decisions made in silence.

Leading while building the clinic required emotional maturity that developed slowly and often painfully. It meant learning to balance responsibility with wisdom, staying steady when the load grew heavier than expected, and trusting God when answers were not immediate. Leadership requires carrying the vision when others cannot yet see it. It demands protecting the assignment from discouragement, distraction, and doubt.

It means standing in a space where faith and reality collide, where pressure reveals character, and where obedience becomes the only option. Leadership calls a person to grow beyond who they once were and step into who they must become.

It was no longer a dream that lived only in conversation or prayer. It became a mission that required time, strategy, planning, and sacrifice. I realized quickly that vision without action is nothing more than hope, and hope without execution fails to produce change. The blueprint forming in front of me challenged who I was and who I was becoming. It required maturity, responsibility, and a willingness to move beyond comfort into unfamiliar territory.

I studied how clinics are built, how healthcare systems function, and how to create operational frameworks strong enough to sustain growth. This work was not glamorous. It was quiet, mentally demanding, and deeply stretching. Some days progress felt invisible, yet every completed line, chart, and plan became another brick placed in a foundation that would one day support real walls, real rooms, and lives transformed.

Each night ended with the understanding that obedience mattered more than comfort. The vision demanded consistency even when energy was depleted and the path ahead felt overwhelming. Leadership forces attention toward the future even when the present feels uncertain. It requires commitment long before results appear. It means standing firm in silence and trusting God beyond logic, emotion, and circumstance.

What I had not fully understood before this journey was that building something for the future requires building yourself first. The blueprint for the clinic required a blueprint for my own life. Discipline had to be strengthened. Focus had to be sharpened. Priorities had to be refined, and thinking had to be restructured. Distractions were eliminated. Time was reorganized. Personal growth was no longer optional. It became essential.

The decisions made in silence shaped every step of the physical building process. I came to understand that God was not only building a clinic. He was building the character required to sustain it. Before any structure could rise from the ground, a foundation had to be formed within me, one that pressure could not break and responsibility could not collapse.

My responsibility was to prepare, plan, and build with excellence. The outcome belonged to God. The timing belonged to God. The resources belonged to God. The breakthrough belonged to God. When responsibility felt overwhelming, that truth became strength. When progress felt slow or unseen, it became fuel. God was shaping the foundation long before the structure appeared, and nothing done in obedience is ever wasted.

The blueprint became more than paper. It became a living assignment. I began meeting with professionals who offered insight and expertise. Conversations with medical staff, business leaders, architects, and healthcare advisors added clarity and direction. Each discussion contributed to a more defined and focused plan.

Every step forward confirmed that God was orchestrating alignment behind the scenes. Though everything was still in development, progress became undeniable. What once felt like a dream began taking shape, piece by piece. I came to understand that God often builds silently before He moves visibly. He prepares in private long before He reveals things publicly.

Leadership requires learning how to balance compassion with strategy, emotion with logic, and patience with urgency. People often reach out broken, tired, or desperate for guidance, strength, and direction. Their pain becomes part of the weight leadership must carry, and their hope becomes part of the assignment that must be protected.

Many conversations required speaking life into places that felt lifeless, offering encouragement when giving up seemed easier, and believing for others when they struggled to believe for themselves. Carrying responsibility for people shapes the heart differently. It teaches the importance of listening deeply rather than reacting quickly, offering understanding rather than judgment, and responding with patience instead of pressure. Leadership grounded in compassion transforms purpose into service and calling into sacrifice.

Serving others while building the clinic deepened my understanding of endurance. There were long nights when the emotional weight felt heavy. People depend on leadership to carry hope, and when someone entrusts you with their struggles, you are holding something sacred. That trust must be protected. Vulnerability must be honored. Pain must be carried with care.

Leadership demands emotional strength that cannot come from human ability alone. It must come from God. There were days when I poured into others while working quietly behind the scenes to build something far greater than anyone could see. That balance between serving and building developed a level of maturity no classroom could teach.

One of the greatest revelations came as I learned the importance of rest. Leaders often believe that relentless movement is necessary, but progress without rest leads to self-destruction. For a long time, I believed that stopping meant falling behind. I believed that stepping away signaled weakness. Over time, I learned that rest is not quitting. Rest is strategy. Rest honors God by refusing to carry what only He can hold.

Rest protects the assignment. Rest restores clarity. Rest strengthens vision. Christ Himself withdrew from crowds to pray and recharge, demonstrating that rest is essential for those called to carry responsibility. Learning to step back allowed me to move forward with greater strength. It taught me that endurance is not measured by how long you push, but by how well you balance effort and recovery.

Silence became a training ground for wisdom. Pressure became a classroom for growth. Responsibility became a catalyst for transformation. The blueprint for the clinic became proof that God develops leaders before He develops projects. He builds hearts before He builds structures. He strengthens foundations before He raises walls. He prepares the vessel before releasing the assignment fully into their hands. Everything being built required discipline, sacrifice, humility, and determination. There were no shortcuts. There were no quick answers. There was only work, faith, patience, and obedience.

Looking ahead, the future no longer feels distant or theoretical. It feels near. It feels tangible. It feels alive. Each day, the weight of destiny grows heavier, not because the burden is overwhelming, but because the purpose is becoming clearer. The blueprint is ready. The foundation is forming. The mission is active.

The journey has moved from survival into construction, from planning into execution, and from quiet endurance into visible advancement. Nothing about this vision is accidental. Every step that led here was necessary. Every struggle was preparation. Every moment of silence built strength. Every sacrifice cleared the path forward.

Before support appears, God often asks a person to invest what they already have. I poured into the vision using my own savings, my own investments, and everything I had gathered from years of disciplined financial sacrifice. It was not easy watching money leave faster than it returned, especially without visible results, but I understood something critical: seeds must leave your hand long before the harvest reaches it. Buildings are not built with imagination. They are built with sacrifice.

The search for land became one of the most demanding phases of planning. It required countless hours researching zoning requirements, medical facility restrictions, and construction regulations. Each potential location came with different challenges: some were well-positioned geographically but lacked utilities; others were affordable but legally complicated.

I drove road after road, walked property after property, and studied land reports late into the night until my eyes burned. Many locations seemed promising at first, only to reveal problems that would cause months of delay and significant financial loss. There were moments when I thought I had finally found the right property, only to discover obstacles that forced the process back to zero. Yet every setback taught me something essential:

purpose requires precision. God does not allow the wrong location to become permanent, no matter how perfect it appears from the outside.

The financial planning required hours of calculations, forecasting, comparing lender requirements, and studying interest structures. I met with banks, commercial lenders, and private investors, only to discover that many doors remain closed until progress becomes visible. The world invests in results, not ideas.

Some conversations ended abruptly; others sounded promising but dissolved without explanation. Every meeting demanded preparation, document packages, business plans, development timelines, projected revenue structures, and sustainability models. These were not just numbers on paper, they were lifelines, representing strategy, vision, and responsibility aligned into structure. Each conversation strengthened my ability to articulate what God had placed in my heart, and each closed door refined clarity instead of destroying hope.

I learned that building requires managing tension: the tension between believing what God said and confronting the reality of obstacles that stand in the way. It required looking at financial numbers that didn't yet make sense and still saying, "This will be built." It meant learning how to communicate vision in boardrooms where people cared more about risk than calling.

It demanded discipline to keep moving even when every circumstance suggested slowing down. Through that pressure, a deeper understanding formed: God does not develop leaders in comfortable places. He shapes them in situations where obedience demands strength beyond human ability.

Prayers alone cannot build structures. Prayer gives direction, but planning builds capacity. I spent endless nights comparing architectural designs, studying how medical centers allocate space for clinics, labs, counseling offices, and emergency rooms. I researched equipment needed for each department, from basic examination supplies to advanced diagnostic tools.

I analyzed staffing models and calculated long-term sustainability, ensuring the clinic would stand not only through excitement but also through seasons of financial tension. I studied insurance partnerships, billing systems, and nonprofit medical models to understand how to create a structure that would operate with integrity, excellence, and long-term impact. Purpose demands intelligence. Vision requires knowledge. Dreams must be translated into structure, or they remain imagination rather than reality.

In the middle of these stages, one truth became undeniably clear: obedience requires proof before evidence appears. Each time fear whispered that the project was too large, too expensive, or too unrealistic, the vision whispered back that impossibility is the birthplace of God's work. The emotional weight was real, but so was the conviction that this mission would save lives long after I am gone. Building something that matters always costs something that feels expensive at the time. Sacrifice becomes the currency that opens the future.

I had never fully understood before that the blueprint is not only the design of the building. The blueprint is also the design of the builder. Every delay shaped patience. Every obstacle shaped strategy. Every financial decision shaped discipline. Every closed door shaped resilience. What felt like waiting was construction happening within me.

God was not building a clinic alone. He was building the leader who would carry it. Now, as the structural details continue to unfold, I stand with a quiet certainty that did not exist before. I may not yet see walls rising from the ground, but I see something even more important: a foundation being formed through decisions, sacrifices, partnerships, planning, and growth.

When the building stands, no one will know the cost except God. That cost is what gives the vision meaning. It proves that faith is real. It proves that purpose demands perseverance. It confirms that God equips those He calls. Dreams begin on paper, but eventually they must move into the real world.

The next stage required movement, strategic and physical movement beyond research and into action. It meant stepping into unfamiliar environments, asking difficult questions, and learning systems I had never navigated before. It required putting faith into motion.

I began studying zoning laws, property requirements, and regulations that determine where a medical facility can be built. I contacted city offices, real estate professionals, and development authorities, not because resources were already available, but because preparation requires positioning. I visited potential areas, learning how location affects accessibility and impact. The process revealed how many decisions must align long before the first wall can be raised. Each conversation became a seed that will one day grow into physical reality.

Financing also moved to the forefront of the mission. The vision was far too large to be carried by personal strength alone. I researched business credit, healthcare funding programs, commercial loan structures, construction financing, and investor partnerships. None of these steps were glamorous. They required early mornings filled with documents, afternoons spent in meetings, and evenings reviewing numbers repeatedly. Many people do not realize that purpose demands administration. Vision must be translated into spreadsheets, budgets, and proposals. Faith does not remove structure. Faith builds it.

There were moments when financial uncertainty pressed hard against the plan. It is one thing to believe when resources already exist. It is another thing to trust God when every step forward requires faith that has not yet seen the outcome. Some nights I stared at spreadsheets, wondering how something so large could ever be funded. Yet the same God who gave the vision is the God who provides provision.

Proverbs 16:3 (NIV) became an anchor during that season: "Commit to the Lord whatever you do, and he will establish your plans." That scripture reminded me that God does not ask us to fund what He calls us to build. He asks us to move in obedience while He arranges the opportunities. My responsibility was preparation. His responsibility was manifestation. With each step, that understanding replaced fear with expectation.

One of the greatest discoveries in this phase was the power of relationships. God began sending the right people at the right time, medical professionals, financial advisers, community leaders, and potential partners who believed before evidence existed. Nothing was promised, and nothing was guaranteed, but every conversation carried momentum.

Doors began opening in places where I expected rejection. Wisdom arrived through voices I never planned to meet. Guidance flowed through people who had walked this road before and understood the landscape. Preparation met favor, and suddenly the future felt closer than ever.

The process taught me something essential: purpose does not begin when the building stands. Purpose begins the moment you move. The work being done today is foundation, not concrete foundation, but spiritual, strategic, and relational foundation. The clinic may not yet exist physically, but its structure is already rising through planning, positioning, and persistence. Faith is learning to celebrate progress that others cannot yet see.

What God is constructing is not a building alone. He is building capacity. He is building discipline. He is building partnerships. He is building influence. Before walls can rise, the builder must rise. Before doors can open, character must be strengthened. Before patients walk in, purpose must be prepared to carry the weight.

And so, the journey continues, not in waiting, but in movement. Not in anxiety, but in expectation. Not in doubt, but in confidence.

It represents movement instead of waiting, service instead of silence, and compassion instead of delay. A mobile unit allows care to travel directly to communities where transportation is limited, where families cannot reach hospitals, and where gaps in the medical system leave entire neighborhoods without support. It transforms waiting time into working time and preparation into action. It ensures that the mission is not only envisioned, but practiced.

To develop the mobile clinic, I began researching medical vans, licensing requirements, retrofitting options, and the costs associated with transforming a vehicle into a fully equipped medical space capable of screenings, health education, and basic services. I learned about partnership opportunities with nurses, physicians, and community providers willing to volunteer their time and skills so families could receive care even before the building exists.

This step is not simply practical. It is spiritual. It is a declaration that the vision will not sit idle while waiting for perfection. God calls us to move with what we have while He prepares what we cannot yet see.

Zechariah 4:10 (NIV) declares, "Do not despise these small beginnings, for the Lord rejoices to see the work begin." The mobile clinic is exactly that, a beginning. A seed planted in faith that will grow into something far greater.

The mobile clinic also serves another purpose: it builds relationships with the community long before the doors of the permanent facility open. It allows people to see that the mission is not theoretical or distant. It is real. It is active. It is present. When a community sees a vision serving them before it stands in brick and concrete, trust is built. Faith is strengthened. Support grows. Most importantly, lives are impacted. A van may not carry the full capacity of a permanent facility, but it carries the heart of the mission: access, compassion, dignity, and hope.

The dream of the clinic is large, but every strong structure begins with smaller steps that establish stability. The mobile unit is Phase One of the larger assignment. It prepares the ground spiritually, relationally, and practically. It provides evidence that God is working through movement and that the future is taking shape now.

When the permanent building opens, it will not mark the beginning of something new. It will be the expansion of something already alive. God is writing a story that does not start at the ribbon cutting. It begins here, in planning, perseverance, strategy, research, partnerships, the mobile clinic, and the decision to serve while building. The foundation is not only concrete. It is obedience. And obedience always builds what vision will one day reveal.

CHAPTER 16

THE SEARCH FOR SACRED GROUND

The search for land became one of the most defining stages of this journey. It began with excitement and a sense of momentum, but as time passed, the process deepened in ways I did not expect. What first seemed like a straightforward task quickly revealed itself as a spiritual assignment, one that required endurance, clarity, and emotional strength.

The process became a teacher, shaping character more than strategy and requiring surrender more than certainty. What I once believed would be completed quickly unfolded slowly, intentionally, and purposefully. Over time, I came to understand that God was not only preparing land. He was preparing me.

In the early phase of the search, I spent long hours driving through different regions, studying maps, reviewing zoning guidelines, and exploring neighborhoods that might support the vision. Some days were filled with anticipation and hope. Other days ended in silence, frustration, and unanswered questions. I walked across open fields imagining buildings rising from the soil, children receiving care, families arriving in peace, and an atmosphere of healing filling every room.

More than once, obstacles appeared without warning. Legal restrictions, environmental barriers, structural limitations, or financial risks made it impossible to move forward. Each time, momentum seemed to collapse suddenly. What looked promising in the morning unraveled by nightfall, and every setback pressed deeper into the discipline of patience.

As the search continued, the emotional weight became impossible to ignore. There were days when the silence felt louder than defeat itself, when hope felt fragile, and when uncertainty pressed heavily against the vision. I remember sitting in my car after another potential location fell through, staring through the windshield as questions swirled. Did I misunderstand God? Was the assignment too large? Had I reached beyond what my ability could sustain?

Those internal battles were more difficult than any external challenge. Yet even then, something within me refused to let go. A quiet conviction remained, insisting that the promise was worth the struggle and that persistence would eventually reveal what waiting was producing.

In the middle of the search, something unexpected happened. A shift occurred, not in the land, but in me. My prayers changed.

Instead of asking God to open a door quickly, I began asking Him to close every door that did not carry His favor. Instead of pleading for speed, I prayed for wisdom. Instead of seeking the easiest path, I sought the right one. I learned to pray not for what felt convenient, but for what carried purpose. I asked God to remove me from any direction that could damage the assignment or weaken its impact. I stopped praying for answers and began praying for alignment. Slowly, peace replaced pressure.

During this time, the team supporting the mission abroad worked tirelessly. They walked the property repeatedly, spoke with local leaders, evaluated safety, examined access routes, and gathered vital information. They invested time, energy, and sacrifice without expecting recognition.

They searched across unfamiliar terrain and uncertain conditions because they believed in the mission and the lives it would affect.

Their commitment revealed an important truth: purpose is not built alone. It is carried through unity. Their dedication reassured me that the vision did not belong to one person. It belonged to everyone willing to invest in something greater than themselves.

I mention them here because their loyalty deserves recognition. On one occasion, while reviewing land options in Haiti, they stood in rain and mud for hours measuring boundaries and assessing potential. Although that location was ultimately eliminated due to risk, their dedication strengthened my resolve. Their persistence became confirmation that the search was worth continuing.

As weeks turned into months, hope shifted. Desperation gave way to determination. Fear was replaced with clarity. I began to understand that the land already existed within God's plan, appointed long before I began searching. We were not trying to create something from nothing. We were moving toward what God had already prepared. Every document reviewed, every conversation held, every obstacle faced, and every disappointment endured brought us closer to the moment of possession. Something internal shifted, and I sensed that we had moved from wandering into alignment. The search became less about chasing something distant and more about approaching something inevitable.

The journey is still unfolding, but the direction is clear. We are closer now than ever before. The foundation is stronger, the strategy is clearer, and the conviction is deeper. Property with real potential has emerged, and for the first time, the land no longer feels theoretical. It feels tangible. It feels within reach. It feels aligned. While additional due diligence remains, the peace surrounding it speaks louder than any obstacle. I cannot yet declare the search complete, but I can declare this: we are standing at the edge of breakthrough.

The weight of the building became even more real when the financial side entered the picture. Building a clinic requires more than inspiration; it requires sacrifice. Every decision carried consequences. Every investment represented a seed planted without visible harvest. When resources stretched thin, the impact felt heavier because the sacrifice was personal. Yet I understood clearly that God was calling me to build something that would outlive me. Legacies are rarely built easily. They are formed through pressure that shapes character stronger than concrete.

The search entered a new phase when serious opportunities emerged. For the first time, land options appeared with real potential. The photographs, measurements, and descriptions brought a different kind of hope. Instead of imagination, it felt like direction. Instead of possibility, it felt like progress.

Even as doors began to open, obstacles appeared just as quickly, a reminder that advancement often attracts resistance. Negotiations stalled without warning. Ownership documents conflicted. Financial details shifted unexpectedly. Every step forward introduced another layer of challenge. It became clear that this journey would require not only conviction, but courage.

During that season, something shifted within me. I began waking with a sense of acceleration, as if the ground beneath my feet was moving. Progress remained quiet, but momentum was undeniable. Each step carried greater weight. Each decision felt closer to fulfillment. The vision stopped feeling distant and began to feel near, close enough to sense, yet still requiring faith to reach. I could feel the transition from preparation toward possession.

We are now standing in a defining moment. The land search is not complete, but it is approaching a turning point. Breakthrough can be sensed before it is seen. Everything that led to this moment was necessary. Every delay protected the mission. Every obstacle produced growth. Every closed door redirected us toward the right path. Every sacrifice laid the foundation for what is preparing to manifest.

That is where I found myself in the land search, standing in a space where the promise felt close, where the weight of destiny pressed forward even though manifestation had not yet appeared. Each step became more intentional. Each conversation carried the potential to change everything. Every decision felt like preparation rather than pressure. Something deep within me awakened, a certainty that could no longer be shaken, a conviction that the land was no longer a question of possibility, but of divine timing.

I realized that breakthroughs rarely occur loudly. They rarely arrive with celebration or visible signs announcing their approach. More often, they come quietly, through unnoticed, ordinary steps that accumulate into supernatural fulfillment. They emerge through subtle shifts that only the spirit can detect. They arrive through peace that defies logic, through direction that feels divinely orchestrated rather than strategically planned.

Because of that, I learned to trust stillness as much as activity. I learned to value quiet movement as much as visible progress. I came to understand that invisible progress is often the most powerful kind, because what God builds in silence becomes unshakable when it is revealed.

The responsibility that once pressed against my chest with anxiety began to settle as purpose, resting firmly within my spirit. I saw clearly that the search for land was never only about purchasing property. It was about becoming the kind of leader capable of carrying the miracle once it arrived. It was about expanding capacity, not just territory.

It was about developing spiritual strength capable of withstanding resistance, criticism, uncertainty, and warfare. God was shaping the architect before shaping the building. He was strengthening character before expanding responsibility. He was preparing the vessel before pouring out the blessing. I began to understand that divine assignments do not depend on circumstances; they depend on endurance. They do not require comfort; they require conviction.

As we now stand closer than ever to securing the land, I feel a peace that surpasses understanding. The right location will not require manipulation or force. It will not produce confusion or hesitation. It will carry the unmistakable signature of God: clarity, unity, peace, confirmation, and favor.

When the moment comes, we will step onto that ground with complete certainty, knowing that every tear, every hour of research, every setback, every disappointment, and every moment of persistent faith prepared us for that single moment when promise becomes reality. We will walk on soil where generations will find healing. We will stand on land where transformation unfolds and testify that God completes what He begins. The miracle will not feel accidental. It will feel appointed.

With that clarity, the work shifted from emotional endurance to technical precision. The search narrowed. Properties were no longer evaluated by hope alone, but by feasibility, sustainability, and long-term protection of the mission. Each conversation became more focused. Each document carried greater weight. The process moved from exploration into stewardship, where every decision bore responsibility for generations beyond my own.

From that point forward, the search was no longer driven by urgency, but by confidence. The pace slowed, not because momentum was lost, but because discernment had matured. We were no longer chasing possibilities.

We were evaluating alignment. The process entered its final posture: readiness.

As the search intensified, it shifted from general exploration into strategic evaluation. We began assessing not only open space, but infrastructure, access to utilities, road connections, legal boundaries, water sources, and long-term viability for expansion. Every property required careful analysis, and each one revealed challenges that demanded wisdom to navigate.

One property appeared ideal at first glance, positioned near a main route that could serve surrounding communities. However, further research revealed unresolved inheritance disputes among family members listed as co-owners. Entering that situation could have resulted in years of legal battles and uncertainty. Walking away was painful, but necessary.

Another location looked promising because of its elevation and layout, which offered natural drainage essential for medical facility construction. However, after surveying the land, the team discovered that the access road belonged to a private owner who refused to grant passage rights. Without legal road access, development would have been impossible.

A third option presented wide open acreage with potential for expansion, but deeper soil testing revealed environmental instability that would have required extensive foundational reinforcement, costing more than the property itself. At first, each rejection felt like a loss. Over time, however, understanding deepened: not every good option is a God option.

We evaluated areas with nearby electrical infrastructure, transportation accessibility, emergency entry points, stormwater drainage, and reliable clean water sources required for medical equipment and sanitation. Conversations with surveyors, attorneys, and local officials filled long days and even longer nights.

Some estimates required more resources than we could responsibly commit. Some negotiations collapsed moments before agreement seemed possible. Other opportunities dissolved without explanation. The process felt like climbing a mountain that continued to rise the closer we climbed. At the same time, it revealed how critical details are to sustaining an operation intended to serve generations.

One of the most challenging aspects of the journey was balancing vision with wisdom. Emotion urged immediate decisions, but responsibility required restraint. The pressure to secure land quickly conflicted with the discipline to wait for confirmation. Each setback demanded deeper humility. Each restart sharpened discernment, and each obstacle stripped away urgency driven by emotion rather than wisdom.

The team reviewed blueprints, researched projected community growth, considered emergency response accessibility, and evaluated how natural disasters could affect long-term use. Nothing about the search was random or casual. It was intentional, strategic, prayerful, and rooted in stewardship rather than impulse. What appeared to be delays were layers of protection.

In one instance, we spent weeks investigating a promising property that seemed perfectly positioned. The size was ideal, road frontage was strong, and community access appeared favorable. However, further investigation revealed that the land sat in a flood-prone zone, requiring costly infrastructure simply to stabilize the foundation. Choosing that property would have compromised the safety of the very people we were called to serve. Walking away was emotionally difficult, yet spiritually freeing. The process reinforced a critical lesson: a leader must be willing to release what looks good in order to receive what is right.

Those experiences trained my eye to see differently. The focus shifted from surface excitement to structural truth. I realized that the land we are seeking cannot simply accommodate buildings; it must support purpose. It must remain strong through storms, time, and expansion. It must be positioned to serve not only present needs, but future generations who will walk through its doors long after I am gone.

That realization transformed the search from a race into a calling. It taught me that what God builds must be engineered with foresight, protected with wisdom, and grounded in a foundation capable of withstanding pressure.

There were days when the weight of responsibility felt heavier than anything I had carried before. I could feel the tension between expectation and reality pressing from every side. Yet it was in those moments, the quiet hours when no answers appeared and no progress was visible, that God reminded me who the true builder was. I began to understand that success would not come from perfect planning or flawless strategy, but from unwavering obedience. Strength would not come from striving, but from surrender.

Breakthrough would not come through force, but through alignment. That realization released a peace that strategy alone could never produce. Faith became the anchor that held firm under pressure, and purpose became the compass directing each step into the unknown.

I now recognize that the search for land has become more than a pursuit of property. It has become a declaration of faith and a testimony unfolding one page at a time. It became the place where God proved that delay is not defeat and waiting is not wasted time. Every obstacle was preparation. Every setback was protection. Every disappointment was divine redirection.

Now, standing in the tension between what is and what will be, certainty rises. God is leading us to the right place, at the right time, with the right people, for the right purpose. We are closer now than ever before. The ground is already chosen. The promise is already written. All that remains is the moment when faith becomes fulfillment and vision becomes reality.

One aspect of the land search that many people rarely recognize is how detailed and technical the process becomes once it moves beyond initial excitement. It is not simply a matter of viewing open space and imagining buildings rising from the soil. Every potential property requires extensive investigation. Survey records must be verified. Boundary lines must be legally confirmed, not assumed visually.

Government offices must be contacted to determine zoning classifications, land-use restrictions, future development limitations, utility access, and environmental conditions that could either support the project or prevent construction altogether. Each site demands hours of research far beyond what can be seen by stepping onto the land.

Some properties require soil testing to determine whether the foundation can support the weight of a medical facility. Others need confirmation of rights-of-way and road access to ensure safe entry for emergency vehicles and community members. Power-line easements, underground water routes, and flood maps must be examined carefully. I learned quickly that land is not simply land.

Every acre carries history, limitations, and possibilities. A property can appear perfect visually yet harbor legal obstacles invisible to the eye. It became necessary to search through records at local municipal offices, review documents with attorneys, consult surveyors, and verify ownership titles to avoid stepping into disputes that could derail the project years later.

In several cases, properties that seemed ideal carried unresolved land title conflicts dating back decades. Signatures were missing, boundaries were contested, or ownership was divided among families no longer communicating. Some parcels required clarification through probate records, which could take months to resolve.

Others revealed hidden liens or government claims that could have jeopardized the project financially. In each situation, hours of labor led to difficult decisions to walk away, not because the land was unappealing, but because pursuing it would place the mission at long-term risk. Turning away from properties that appeared perfect was painful, but wisdom demanded discipline over excitement.

At one point, the team spent days gathering documentation for a property that carried enormous promise, only to discover an environmental restriction requiring an expensive remediation process due to prior land use. The numbers continued to be prohibitive.

Another property revealed a lack of access to reliable water infrastructure, which would have required drilling a deep commercial well with no guarantee of success. The emotional weight of letting go of promising land was heavy, not because of lost opportunity, but because each new beginning reopened the grind of research, calls, meetings, calculations, and prayer.

Yet these challenges shaped a deeper understanding: purpose is not fragile. Purpose survives elimination. Purpose survives rejection. Purpose survives research that leads to closed doors. The right land will not collapse under scrutiny. It will withstand investigation, legal confirmation, and technical examination. God-ordained ground does not require compromise or desperation. It carries clarity.

Each obstacle forced the development of skills that would later become essential: evaluating contracts, analyzing land assessments, requesting GIS mapping, negotiating with property owners, deciphering legal terminology, and holding conversations with engineers, surveyors, and attorneys. Nothing about the process was glamorous, but everything about it was necessary. Purpose demands stewardship, not emotion. Structure comes before celebration. Foundation comes before framing.

Nothing visibly changed. No new property appeared. No unexpected phone call came through. No document was signed. Yet something inside transformed. It was as if the atmosphere around the vision had shifted.

I woke with a sense of certainty I had not felt before, a stillness carrying more strength than excitement ever could. It felt like alignment, as though something unseen had moved into position.

For months, I had carried a weight pressing against my chest like stone. But that morning, the weight lifted, replaced by a peace so deep I could feel it in my breathing. I realized that God had shifted the battle, not externally, but internally. The war that once raged in the mind had moved into quiet victory in the spirit.

At that moment, I understood something years of waiting had been preparing me to learn: the promise does not begin when the land is purchased. The promise begins when peace arrives. Peace is evidence that heaven has already spoken. Peace is proof that breakthrough has already begun. Peace is the confirmation that the process has shifted from searching to positioning. I recognized that we were now standing not at the beginning of pursuit, but at the threshold of fulfillment.

It was clear the search had moved beyond wandering and entered alignment. I no longer felt the pressure of uncertainty. Instead, there was boldness, confidence, and a settled assurance that the right land was already appointed, already secured spiritually, already sealed in heaven. All that remained was stepping into what God had already determined.

In that season, God taught me that faith is not proven in celebration. It is proven in the decisions we make in silence. Faith is not proven on the mountaintop, but in the valley where no applause exists and no progress is visible. Faith is proven when nothing moves and yet we refuse to stop moving. I began to understand that the quietest seasons are often the most defining, because they reveal who truly believes.

Faith built in stillness is unbreakable. Confidence built without physical evidence cannot be shaken by circumstances. That revelation changed everything. I stopped evaluating progress by results and began measuring it by preparation. I stopped looking outward and started building inward. Something in me grew. Something in me expanded. Something in me strengthened. Searching for land had become the tool God used to construct the leader required to steward the promise.

I realized that the land search was not meant to break me; it was meant to build me. It was forming patience stronger than pressure, vision stronger than distraction, obedience stronger than fear, and confidence stronger than uncertainty. The same process that once felt like a burden became the ground where faith matured.

And now, standing at this moment in the story, I know without hesitation that the land is coming. The key will be placed in our hands. The promise will become physical. The doors will open, and the soil will be claimed. It will not come through struggle or force, it will come in God's perfect timing.

It will come through divine timing, wrapped in supernatural peace. And when we stand on the ground God has ordained, the journey that once felt exhausting will become the testimony that strengthens those who come after us. What once looked like delay will be revealed as preparation. What once looked like silence will be revealed as strategy. And what once looked like waiting will be revealed as the foundation of faith that made the assignment unshakeable.

CHAPTER 17

THE WAR AROUND
THE VISION

The most intense battles of this journey did not take place silently within my own mind. They appeared outwardly, rising like storms the moment real progress began to take shape. When the land search moved from possibility into reality, the resistance increased in ways I had never experienced before. Doors that once opened easily began closing without reason. Promising conversations that seemed stable suddenly shifted direction. Negotiations that appeared clear became complicated overnight.

Systems that once supported progress began producing obstacles I was not sure I possessed the strength to overcome. It became clear that the resistance was not coincidental. It was a confrontation. It was warfare surrounding what God intended to build. The battle did not form because of what I had already achieved; it formed because of what was coming. I realized that spiritual warfare often intensifies the moment destiny begins to move. Progress awakens opposition.

The Lord reminded me of Nehemiah. When Nehemiah began rebuilding the wall assigned by God, the enemy immediately tried to stop the work. Nehemiah 4:17 (NIV) reads, "Those who carried materials did their work with one hand and held a weapon in the other." That scripture revealed something profound: building what God commands requires more than vision. It requires warfare. It requires carrying responsibility in one hand and spiritual discipline in the other.

Nehemiah could not stop building simply because the enemy hated what he was constructing. Instead, he adjusted his posture. He strengthened his resolve. He continued building while defending the assignment at the same time. The wall did not fall because resistance appeared; it stood because determination refused to bow. That scripture became instructions for this journey. It reminded me that opposition is not a sign to stop. It is a sign to guard the mission and keep building.

The resistance surrounding the land search became undeniable. Every time progress advanced, something attempted to interfere. Documents were delayed for reasons no one could explain. Meetings were canceled moments before they were scheduled to begin. Legal clarity shifted back into uncertainty without warning. Opportunities that seemed certain dissolved unexpectedly.

The weight of those moments felt heavy enough to suffocate determination. And yet, something inside refused to give up. I understood then that the battle was not against people or circumstances. It was spiritual. Ephesians 6:12 (NIV) declares, "For our struggle is not against flesh and blood, but against the rulers, against the authorities, against the powers of this dark world and against the spiritual forces of evil in the heavenly realms."

That truth changed everything. It shifted my focus from frustration to strategy. I stopped viewing resistance as a personal attack and began seeing it as evidence. The intensity of the warfare revealed the magnitude of the assignment. The enemy does not fight what poses no threat. He fights what is destined to break chains and heal generations.

During this season, I discovered that progress demands protection. Growth requires spiritual strength. Purpose requires vigilance. I learned to build naturally through meetings, planning, documents, and negotiations, while fighting spiritually through prayer, worship, and unwavering faith. There were days when the only breakthrough happened internally rather than externally.

God was not only protecting the future land; He was training my spirit to withstand the responsibility the land would carry. I learned that the true test of faith is not how loudly you can shout when everything is moving forward. The true test is how steady you remain when everything stands still.

The pressure was real. At times, it felt relentless. But pressure does not come to destroy; it comes to reveal strength that would not surface any other way. Pressure forced me to pray differently. Pressure forced me to listen more carefully. Pressure forced me to depend on God in a way that strategy alone could never replace. Through every setback, something deep within me grew stronger.

I realized that spiritual warfare is not proof that God is absent. It is proof that destiny is near. Whenever God prepares to release something significant, resistance intensifies and the battlefield expands. The enemy was not fighting land. He was fighting legacy. He was fighting families whose lives would be changed. He was fighting children who will one day experience healing. He was fighting generations whose stories will not end in suffering.

I understand that warfare was necessary. It produced endurance that no classroom could teach. It built resilience that no textbook could provide. It strengthened faith that no sermon could replace. It created the internal foundation required before any physical foundation could be laid in the soil. The spiritual battle did not break the vision. It validated it. It proved that what we are building is not ordinary. It proved that what is coming is significant. And it proved that the promise will not be stopped.

The spiritual warfare intensified when the process reached the level of government involvement. What had once been a matter of research and discernment quickly turned into a maze of regulations, paperwork, approvals, and unexpected financial demands. Each new step revealed another requirement, another signature, another document that needed verification before the project could advance. Meetings that should have taken minutes turned into hours.

Processes that were explained as simple became complicated without warning. Information that should have been clear arrived fragmented and confusing. It felt as though progress was being intentionally slowed, as though invisible hands were working to delay movement. The pressure did not come only through spiritual resistance; it appeared through systems and structures that held authority over the land. There were moments when it seemed as if the process was designed to create exhaustion and test the strength of the vision.

At one point, we were required to settle unexpected administrative fees before any further steps could be taken. These were not small amounts that could be paid casually. They represented sacrifices that required prayer, planning, and careful stewardship. Yet there was no alternative. Without submitting payment, the process would halt completely, and everything we had invested up to that point would become immobile.

I remember standing in that moment, wrestling with the weight of the decision. It felt like a test designed to expose intentions. Would we continue even when the cost increased, or would fear convince us to retreat? I understood that obedience sometimes demands financial sacrifice before breakthroughs appear. The vision had moved beyond inspiration. It now demanded investment. It demanded proof that faith was more than words printed on a page.

The pressure intensified when government offices delayed expected approvals without explanation. Documents were misplaced. Signatures were postponed. Requests were processed and then returned with new requirements that had not been previously mentioned. Phone calls went unanswered. Emails received no reply. Days stretched into weeks, and every delay felt like resistance rising higher.

The stress was no longer just emotional or spiritual, it became financial and structural. There were moments when the process seemed close to collapsing under the weight of bureaucracy, as though the systems themselves were designed to slow anything that threatened to create change. It felt like a battle not just for land, but against structures built to discourage persistence and drain endurance.

During that time, God reminded me of a scripture that strengthened my spirit when discouragement tried to take root. Isaiah 54:17 (NIV) declares, "No weapon forged against you will prevail, and you will refute every tongue that accuses you." That verse shifted everything. It reminded me that weapons may form, but they ultimately fail. It reminded me that resistance would rise, but it would not dominate. It reminded me that every obstacle placed in our path had already been defeated in the eyes of heaven. That scripture became the anchor holding me steady when frustration threatened to erode clarity. It spoke to my spirit each time the process stalled, showing that delays are not denials, delays mean movement is happening in the unseen.

Carrying the vision through government pressure felt like walking uphill while holding weight that increased with every step. Yet even in the pressure, something deeper was forming. I recognized that God was teaching me how to lead under scrutiny, how to stand firm in the face of bureaucracy, and how to protect a mission in environments designed for resistance. Leadership requires the ability to remain steady when systems become overwhelming. It requires discipline to respond to obstacles with strategy instead of panic. It demands patience more strongly than pressure.

Looking back, I now see clearly that the struggle with government processes was not merely a procedural battle. It was training. It was refinement. It was preparation for the authority required once the land is secured. The battle showed me that true faith requires movement even when the path is obstructed. It requires trusting God fully when human systems fail. It requires believing that if God appointed the assignment, then no office, no decision, no paperwork, no fee, and no resistance has the power to stop what heaven has authorized.

The struggle revealed that spiritual warfare does not always manifest as conflict that can be seen. Sometimes it appears in quiet obstacles designed to exhaust belief and weaken determination. But what the enemy used to apply pressure ultimately produced endurance that nothing else could have built. Through it all, I learned that persistence is an act of warfare. Refusing to stop is spiritual combat. Continuing to move forward is victory in motion.

With each barrier faced and overcome, I began to see something remarkable: the pressure was not breaking the assignment, it was shaping it. The attacks were intentional because the impact would be extraordinary. They proved that what we are building carries a weight the enemy fears. Pressure did not crush the vision. It purified it. It separated emotion from conviction. It revealed that the foundation of this mission is not made of fragile dreams but of unshakeable purpose.

When purpose is under construction, the battlefield is rarely external, it is internal. Real war is often fought in silence within the mind, the heart, and the hidden places nobody sees. It begins when doubt whispers questions that challenge certainty. It intensifies when fatigue makes progress feel impossible. It attempts to suffocate belief by surrounding the soul with disappointment and uncertainty. Yet understanding the nature of spiritual warfare changes how the believer responds to it. Scripture teaches that battles connected to destiny cannot be fought with human wisdom or emotional strength alone.

Instead, they require spiritual weapons designed to tear down invisible resistance. Second Corinthians 10:4 (NIV) declares, "The weapons we fight with are not the weapons of the world. On the contrary, they have divine power to demolish strongholds." This reminder carries authority because it reveals that the greatest victories are won not by physical force, but by spiritual discipline. Prayer, worship, obedience, the Word of God, and steadfast endurance are not passive responses, they are military strategies that dismantle the enemy's grip.

Waiting becomes a weapon. Persistence becomes warfare. Endurance becomes testimony. These seasons reveal the depth of faith more clearly than times of visible progress, when everything moves smoothly.

The believer who continues forward despite silence becomes dangerous to the enemy because they demonstrate a level of spiritual maturity that cannot be manipulated by fear or shaken by delay. The enemy cannot defeat someone who refuses to quit.

Every step taken under pressure declares war against darkness. Every decision to press forward amid emotional strain reinforces spiritual authority. Every night of prayer, every tear cried in private, every moment where surrender was resisted builds internal strength capable of carrying blessing without breaking under the weight of responsibility.

Yet even in the tension, something unexplainable happened. The more intense the warfare became, the stronger the conviction inside me grew. A quiet but unshakeable certainty settled like weight in my spirit, declaring that giving up was not an option and retreat was not an alternative. I began to recognize that the pressure was not a signal to stop; it was proof that breakthrough was closer than ever.

That season taught me that obedience requires endurance and that surrender is sometimes the greatest act of strength. It taught me that leadership is not measured by the absence of struggle, but by the refusal to quit in the presence of it. It taught me that when God entrusts a calling that carries generational impact, He also equips resilience capable of surviving seasons of silence, resistance, and delayed answers.

What looked from the outside like waiting was, on the inside, the construction of a foundation strong enough to carry what was coming next. And in that quiet, sacred tension between exhaustion and expectation, faith rose again, steady and unmovable, declaring that the God who began this would finish it.

It settled onto my shoulders in a way heavier than any physical load I had carried before. It was not just the difficulty of the process that pressed against me; it was the awareness that people were waiting, believing, and depending on the fulfillment of a promise God had placed in my heart.

I could feel the responsibility like a constant presence, sitting in the space between vision and reality. The greater the expectation grew, the more silent the process seemed to become. There were moments when I sat in meetings or stood on open land, composed externally while internally grappling with fear that whispered endlessly, questioning whether I was truly equipped to carry what I was fighting to build.

Leadership in seasons of delay requires a strength invisible to the world. It demands composure when uncertainty rises like a storm. It requires the ability to speak peace to others even when peace feels distant internally. I felt that tension sharply. People would ask for updates and timelines, eager to know when the land would be secured. Their hope inspired me, but it also intensified the pressure.

I understood that every decision I made carried real implications for the lives that would one day walk through the doors of the clinic. Many nights I sat staring at scattered papers, reading legal documents, running cost analyses by the dim light of my living room, while silence filled the space like a thick fog. I wondered at times if God was waiting for something in me to break before He moved the next piece into place.

In that season, the battle shifted inward. I confronted thoughts that attempted to erode the very foundation of my calling. The enemy does not attack where nothing is at stake. He attacks purpose, identity, and direction. He targets the mind at the point where faith is most needed. I battled thoughts that questioned my capability, suggested easier alternatives, and tried to convince me that the promise was slipping away. Yet every moment of weakness was countered by a supernatural strength that did not originate from myself.

In that quiet season, something unfamiliar and powerful began to form. Strength rose not from achievement but from endurance. Confidence emerged not from progress but from persistence. The pressure that once felt crushing began shaping me. It carved depth, maturity, focus, and spiritual resilience.

I realized that leadership is often formed in private long before it is recognized in public. God was developing a leader who would not crumble under the weight of the miracle. He was training a warrior who would not retreat when resistance intensified. The internal breakthrough had to happen before the external breakthrough could manifest. And in that revelation, peace finally settled like a calm after a storm.

The breakthrough did not arrive through a sudden announcement or an unexpected phone call. It emerged quietly, almost unnoticed at first, through subtle shifts that gradually began to change the direction of the journey. After months of pressure, uncertainty, unanswered communication, and stalled negotiations, progress began to surface in ways that could only be described as divine alignment.

It started when a door that had remained closed for weeks reopened without explanation, and a contact who once seemed uninterested reached out requesting a conversation. What once required pushing and pleading suddenly moved forward with ease. Meetings that had previously ended in confusion transformed into discussions filled with clarity and cooperation. The rhythm of resistance began turning into momentum, and for the first time in a long time, the energy surrounding the vision felt light rather than heavy.

One of the most significant moments came after an exhausting week of reviewing legal complications regarding potential property. The research had drained my energy and tested my resolve. After countless hours analyzing documents with attorneys and reviewing municipal requirements, I reached the point of emotional surrender.

I remember praying late into the night, placing every frustration and every unanswered question before God, asking Him to close the door firmly if the property was not meant to be. The next morning, the phone rang with information that shifted everything. The complications that once seemed immovable were suddenly resolved. A previously unavailable document surfaced, and an unexpected supporter offered guidance through the legal process. It was not a coincidence. It was confirmation. It was a reminder that when God moves, He does so without strain.

Progress continued to unfold in pieces rather than dramatic leaps. Small victories began accumulating. Papers that had been delayed were processed faster than anticipated. Clarity emerged regarding zoning allowances. Conversations with local leadership shifted from resistance to collaboration. Resources that were uncertain became available. Each step forward carried the quiet weight of divine timing.

I understood then that breakthrough does not always arrive through fire and noise. Often, breakthroughs arrive wrapped in peace. Psalm 32:8 (NIV) says, "I will instruct you and teach you in the way you should go; I will counsel you with my loving eye on you." That scripture carried new meaning as I watched God orchestrate details beyond human ability to influence.

One meeting stands out vividly in my memory. I had walked into the room prepared for another battle, ready to defend the purpose behind the project and to address concerns with patience but firmness. Instead of resistance, I was met with unexpected support. Individuals who once seemed uncertain about allowing the project to move forward expressed interest in becoming part of the process.

Questions that once felt like obstacles became bridges to deeper understanding and collaboration. By the time the meeting ended, the atmosphere had shifted dramatically. It was as if the spiritual resistance that once stood like a wall had crumbled without warning. I walked out of the building with a quiet sense of victory and tears of gratitude welling in my eyes, knowing that every tear shed in private prayer was now being honored in public progress.

The turning point was not defined by the signing of a contract or the exchange of money. It was defined by certainty. It was defined by the realization that we were no longer pushing against a closed door but walking through an opening created by God Himself. The weight that once pressed against my spirit lifted. Pressure transformed into purpose, and the vision that once felt distant took a visible shape before my eyes. For the first time, I felt the land was not only a possibility but a reality. Though the key was not yet in hand, the breakthrough had already happened. The physical manifestation was simply waiting for the appointed time.

This was the moment when the search moved beyond process and into prophecy. Every delay that once felt painful began to make sense. Every setback aligned itself like puzzle pieces forming a larger picture. Every unanswered prayer revealed itself as preparation. The journey had shifted from endurance to expectancy, and the promise was no longer something I was hoping to see, it was something I was preparing to receive. I realized that breakthrough is not only what God does around us. Breakthrough is what God completes within us first. The land was coming. The miracle was already unfolding.

The story of Nehemiah became a mirror to my own journey. Nehemiah had a clear assignment from God to rebuild the walls of Jerusalem, yet the moment he began the work, opposition intensified. He faced mockery, threats, political resistance, and strategic attempts to exhaust and discourage the workers.

It was never the wall alone that the enemy fought. It was what the wall represented. The wall symbolized restoration, identity, protection, and revival for a nation that had suffered for too long. Likewise, the search for land is not simply about property. It represents healing, dignity, and transformation for children and families who have waited far too long for hope. The enemy does not attack what has no value. He attacks what is designed to change lives.

Nehemiah did not respond to the attacks emotionally. He responded spiritually. He prayed, he planned, and he positioned his people to build with a hammer in one hand and a sword in the other. His determination was rooted not in physical strength, but in spiritual conviction.

Every distraction, every delay, every setback, and every challenge has been an invitation to come down, to retreat, to surrender, to accept defeat.

Yet the calling refuses to be silent. Like Nehemiah, I have learned to build and battle at the same time.

This perspective strengthened my resolve during the most challenging days. When discouragement whispered defeat, the mission reminded me that surrender was not an option. When exhaustion weighed heavily, the vision lifted me with a purpose stronger than fatigue.

When silence felt suffocating, the promises of God spoke louder than doubt. Building a legacy requires more than passion. It requires spiritual endurance. It requires the willingness to stand firm when everything around you shakes. It requires the courage to choose faith when fear screams the loudest. It requires perseverance even when clarity seems distant.

Just like the wall Nehemiah built, this clinic is more than a structure. It is a declaration. It is a stand against suffering. It is resistance against generational pain. It is an answer to years of unanswered prayer. It is a place where healing will replace hopelessness, and where lives will be transformed for generations to come. That is why the battle has been fierce. That is why the search has been long. That is why the journey has demanded surrender, sacrifice, and supernatural strength. The fight reveals the value of what is being built.

Now, standing at the edge of breakthrough, the assignment has never been clearer. The battle is not over, but the victory has already begun. The enemy fought because he saw what we could not yet see. He fought because he understood the impact before we experienced it.

As we step into the next stage of this journey, we move not with fear, but with boldness. Not with hesitation, but with confidence. Not with anxiety, but with spiritual authority. The land will be secure. The clinic will be built. The promise will manifest. The testimony will speak. And every battle that attempts to break us will become part of the story that strengthens others.

This journey has taught me to trust God not when the plan is visible, but when the path disappears.

CHAPTER 18

THE POWER OF
UNEXPECTED ALIGNMENT

Breakthrough rarely arrives in the form we expect. It does not always appear with loud celebration or in dramatic moments that announce themselves with obvious clarity. Instead, it often enters quietly, through unexpected people, unforeseen conversations, and opportunities that slip into our lives with such gentle precision that we only recognize their significance in hindsight. After the weight of spiritual warfare, the pressure of delay, and the intensity of the emotional battle that stretched faith nearly to its breaking point, something began to shift.

Alignment first appeared through people whose paths crossed mine in ways too intentional to be coincidence. Individuals I had never met, who knew nothing of the sacrifices, the tears, or the countless hours invested, suddenly stepped forward with insight, strategy, and support that could not have been manufactured through human networking.

The positioning revealed itself through moments that carried the unmistakable signature of divine orchestration. Calls arrived unexpectedly. Scheduling openings appeared after weeks of silence. Opportunities resurfaced when discouragement had nearly convinced me to abandon them. Situations that once required intense effort suddenly moved forward with ease. Government processes that had stalled completely began progressing again. Conversations that once felt confrontational shifted into collaboration. Individuals who once seemed indifferent began advocating passionately.

One moment in particular stands as evidence of alignment at work. After weeks of exhausting negotiations, legal confusion, and halted communication, I walked into a meeting fully braced for conflict. I expected another defensive conversation, another wall, another setback that would demand endurance beyond what remained in my spirit. Instead, the atmosphere shifted the moment I sat down.

The room itself seemed to change. Individuals who had previously approached with caution and skepticism now leaned forward with genuine interest. Their questions moved from confrontation to collaboration. The air carried possibility, and people who had once expressed doubt began offering innovative solutions, their words infused with a renewed sense of hope and purpose.

The conversation flowed effortlessly, like a river finally finding its course. The heavy resistance that had once surrounded the project seemed to dissolve, replaced by an undercurrent of determination and resolve. It was as if the very atmosphere had shifted, allowing the vision to breathe and expand.

As I walked out of the building, tears pricked at the corners of my eyes. I felt a deep awe and gratitude, knowing that something supernatural had just transpired. It was not a victory marked by a signature or a grand announcement, but a quiet, seismic shift in the spiritual realm.

This was the moment when alignment met opportunity, forever changing the trajectory of the project. It proved that breakthroughs do not begin with earthly contracts or tangible achievements, they begin in the unseen realm of the spirit.

When God aligns something, no human resistance can undo it. Alignment is evidence that heaven has already signed what earth has yet to see, a declaration that the outcome is not a question of "if," but "when."

In that moment, I realized the battle had not been won through my own strength or strategy, but through the sovereign power of God. Resistance had been dismantled, not by human hands, but by the gentle yet unyielding force of divine alignment.

The tears I felt were not just tears of joy, they were tears of surrender. I had glimpsed the invisible, and it had changed everything. The journey ahead would still hold challenges, but I knew I was no longer alone, no longer fighting against insurmountable odds.

I was now walking in the wake of God's alignment, certain that the vision would come to pass, not because of my own efforts, but because of the unshakeable promise of the One who had set it in motion. The alignment was undeniable, and with it came a revelation that transformed everything: the miracle had already begun long before the land was secured. The manifestation was already moving toward us. The promise was already in motion. The vision was transitioning from unseen to seen. The land was no longer a distant hope, it was a destination we were being carried toward by God's power and faithfulness.

The more progress emerged, the clearer it became that nothing in this journey was accidental. Every closed door suddenly made sense. Every delay revealed hidden protection. Every disappointment became a doorway redirecting us toward the place where purpose resides. It was as though God Himself had been clearing the path, removing wrong options, blocking unwise partnerships, and dismantling every possibility that would have positioned us outside His timing.

What once felt like resistance now revealed itself as divine safeguarding. What once felt like struggle revealed itself as strategy. What once felt like abandonment revealed itself as a construction zone, where God was building the strength required for all that was coming next.

There is a moment in every journey when the believer sees clearly that God was never silent; He was working. He was never absent; He was arranging. He was never delaying; He was aligning. That realization settled into my spirit like the slow sunrise after a long night, illuminating everything that once seemed confusing.

Some of these moments came in passing, in unexpected places, a parking lot, a restaurant, a brief phone call, yet each carried enough strength to lift days of discouragement. I began to understand that God does not always reveal His plan through dramatic revelation. Sometimes, He speaks through ordinary moments, through simple conversations that carry extraordinary significance.

He speaks quietly through the mouths of people who have no awareness of the Spirit moving through them. I realized that every resource we needed did not appear through searching. It appeared through surrender. It appeared when striving ceased and faith rested. It appeared when focus shifted from fighting to trusting, from pushing to listening, from struggling to aligning. Alignment became evidence that heaven had already said yes.

The deeper the alignment grew, the more I became aware that God was shaping not only the journey but also the capacity of the vessel carrying it. The peace that once felt fragile transformed into confidence rooted beyond emotion. It was a confidence that could not be shaken by delay because it did not come from results, it came from conviction. God does not give peace to confirm completion. He gives peace to confirm direction. That understanding reshaped everything within me.

Pressure no longer felt like a threat; it became a sign that I was standing exactly where God intended. Silence no longer felt like abandonment; it became a place where faith was purified. Resistance no longer felt like failure; it became proof that a breakthrough was near. Everything inside me began to shift from merely surviving the process to embracing it, trusting that nothing being built in this season would be wasted. Even the pain was shaping purpose.

In that place of alignment, God began restoring strength piece by piece. Sleep returned. Clarity returned. Hope returned, not as fleeting excitement or superficial enthusiasm, but as certainty. There were nights when I sat quietly, blueprints and maps spread before me, not with anxiety but with anticipation. For the first time in the journey, I could feel the weight of victory approaching.

It was like the wind shifting direction before a storm breaks, announcing itself without sound. The atmosphere carried a different weight. It felt like standing in a room alive with quiet movement, where unseen activity makes itself known without explanation. It felt as if heaven itself was leaning forward, and creation was preparing to witness what God was about to reveal.

One morning, I woke with a sense of urgency that was neither anxious nor frantic, but intentional and steady. The prompting was unmistakable: something was shifting. I stepped outside, and the air felt different, lighter, as though something in the unseen realm had broken open. I stood still, letting it settle over me. It was not emotion. It was revelation. I felt with certainty that the season of wandering had ended.

The season of searching had shifted into the season of stepping. For the first time, I felt drawn, not to an idea of land, but to a physical location that rose within my spirit with clarity I had never experienced. I could not yet explain it logically. I could not justify it on paper. But the alignment in my spirit was louder than any evidence. It felt like God saying, "Move."

It felt like the moment when faith takes a step, not because certainty is visible, but because obedience recognizes God's voice.

The alignment unfolding around me created a holy anticipation that felt almost tangible. Every part of me understood that we were closer than ever before, not emotionally, but spiritually. Not practically, but prophetically. The land was near. The breakthrough was unfolding. The miracle was already in motion. The journey that had once demanded endurance now invited expectation, and the faith that had once trembled now stood unshakable.

The day came when the alignment within my spirit was too clear to ignore. It was not planned or scheduled. There were no announcements, meetings, or strategy sessions surrounding it. It began quietly, with an inner stirring that felt unmistakably divine. I knew I needed to go. I needed to physically place my feet on the ground that God had been preparing long before I began searching. There was no dramatic trigger, no external cue.

There was simply a still, firm whisper: "Go now."

I got into the car with a calm that felt sacred, driving not with anxiety but with anticipation. Every mile was an act of faith, every turn a step of obedience. I understood in that moment what it means to move without full clarity but with full conviction. I was not following a map, I was following the peace of God.

As the location came into view, something shifted inside me so intensely that it felt as though time slowed. I stepped out of the car, and the air carried a weight I could feel in my chest. The ground beneath my feet felt different, as if the soil itself recognized purpose. I stood silently, looking across the open expanse stretched before me, and something rose within my spirit that defies description.

It felt like home. It felt like stepping onto ground that already belonged to the assignment, even before a contract was signed or a document approved. It was as though God had been waiting, not for me to explore land, but to acknowledge it. Tears filled my eyes, not from exhaustion or struggle, but from the overwhelming awareness that I was standing inside an answered prayer before the answer had fully manifested. I could sense the weight of generations standing with me, children who would one day receive healing, families restored, futures rebuilt, lives saved. It felt like stepping into destiny.

In that quiet moment, I began to walk the perimeter slowly, praying under my breath with a reverence I had never experienced. The wind moved gently through the trees, and the stillness carried confirmation stronger than any voice I had ever heard. It felt as though heaven itself leaned close, surrounding the land like a shield.

A verse came alive in my spirit with such power that my knees weakened. Joshua 1:3 (NIV) declares, "I will give you every place where you set your foot, as I promised Moses." Those words did not feel like history. They felt like prophecy. They felt like God speaking directly into the moment, reminding me that the ground beneath my feet was not random, but appointed. It was proof that the promise did not depend on my strength, it depended on His faithfulness.

I closed my eyes and placed my hand on the soil, letting the dirt rest against my palm. Peace rose like strength. Clarity formed like structure. Purpose stood like a pillar beneath my feet. I remained there silently for a long time, allowing God to settle everything that had once felt heavy. The fear that had battled my mind dissolved. The exhaustion that weighed on my shoulders lifted. The uncertainty that clouded direction vanished like fog under the morning sun. In its place stood certainty.

In its place stood authority. In its place stood faith reborn with a depth I had never known. I realized then that I was not just walking land. I was walking through a prophecy. I was stepping into the physical expression of a promise God had birthed long before I understood the assignment. The waiting had not been in vain. The warfare had not been wasted. Every tear, every night of silence, every stumbling step, every unanswered question had prepared me for this ground.

As I stood there, the future unfolded in my spirit like a vision. I could see the entrance rising. I could see the foundation poured. I could hear the echo of children laughing. I could feel the presence of families arriving, seeking help, hope, and healing. I could see generations stepping onto this land, carrying their pain and walking away restored. In that moment, I understood why the enemy fought so fiercely.

I understood why the resistance was aggressive. I understood why the pressure was unrelenting. He saw what God was building long before I ever touched the soil. He knew the lives that would change before I ever saw the land. He recognized the territory being reclaimed before I even took a step. And now, standing upon the ground God promised, I knew with absolute certainty that nothing could stop what heaven had already authorized.

I walked back to the car slowly, not with the weight I had carried when I arrived, but with victory resting firmly in my chest. I whispered a simple prayer, thanking God not for the land itself, but for the strength He built through the journey that led to it. I understood something I had never fully grasped before: the miracle does not begin when the key is handed over. The miracle begins when faith steps where God directs.

Victory begins when footsteps touch the ground heaven has already claimed. That day, without signatures or announcements, without celebration or witnesses, the promise shifted from belief to possession. The land was no longer a dream. It was a reality waiting on timing.

I drove away knowing with absolute certainty that we were standing at the threshold of fulfillment. Not hoping. Not wondering. Knowing. The next chapter would not be about searching. It would be about securing. It would be about stepping into the manifestation of everything God had prepared through the fire, through the pressure, and through the silence.

Faith does not wait for paperwork. Faith responds when God speaks. Faith celebrates before results appear. Faith stands on the ground that will one day hold the weight of destiny and declares confidently that the future is already written. Psalm 46:10 (NIV) came alive in my heart: "Be still, and know that I am God." That verse was not a command to do nothing, but an invitation to rest in certainty. It was a reminder that striving ends where surrender begins, and that pressure breaks when trust becomes complete.

As the road stretched before me, I felt a growing awareness that the long season of waiting had reached its final stretch. The journey no longer felt like climbing. It felt like arrival. The vision no longer felt like hope. It felt like fulfillment.

I thought of the children whose lives would be transformed, the families who would walk through these doors seeking healing, the communities that would one day speak of restoration born on this ground. I thought of every person who had believed alongside me, every prayer spoken, every seed sown, every word of encouragement poured into weary days.

I thought of generations not yet born who would walk on this land, unaware of the warfare that preceded their healing. And suddenly, I felt the weight of history pressing gently against the present, reminding me that this assignment extends far beyond one lifetime. It is a legacy, a divine inheritance prepared not only for this generation, but for those who will come long after we are gone.

The road home that day felt like a procession of victory in silence. I understood that the real breakthrough had already taken place, and the land would soon transition from promise to possession. A stillness settled deep within me, a stillness that declared boldly that God had finished something in the unseen, and all that remained was timing. The kind of timing that needs no rushing and requires no fear.

The kind of timing that moves mountains without hands and opens doors without knocking. The kind of timing that reveals itself in perfect orchestration, when spirit and purpose meet at the exact intersection heaven has already determined. The miracle was not waiting to be formed. The miracle was waiting to be revealed.

I drove the rest of the way with peace riding beside me like a passenger, wrapping itself around every breath. Strength rose again. Purpose settled firmly. Confidence returned fully. The uncertainty that had once lingered vanished completely. Every question that had demanded an answer fell silent. I knew that I did not need to see what God was doing next in order to trust the outcome.

I simply needed to remain obedient and prepared. The journey had shifted permanently. It was no longer about finding land. It was about receiving what God had already prepared. The war had produced a warrior. The waiting had produced wisdom. The pressure had produced power.

I knew with absolute certainty that this was the beginning of manifestation. The next steps would not be taken in fear, they would be taken in authority. The next decisions would not be made in confusion, they would be made clearly. The next season would not be defined by struggle, it would be defined by fulfillment. The land was coming. The promise was unfolding. The miracle was already alive. And nothing in heaven or earth could stop what God had already placed into motion.

When I returned home that night, the atmosphere inside the house felt transformed. A quiet weight of peace rested over everything, the kind of peace that settles deeply and does not need to announce itself. For the first time in months, my soul felt still. I sat in silence, with no desire to move quickly or analyze the events of the day. Instead of strategizing or replaying conversations in my mind, I simply breathed.

It felt as though God Himself had stepped into the room and removed the burden that had pressed against my spirit. The pressure that once made breathing difficult lifted like fog under sunlight. For the first time in months, I felt fully rested while awake, as though strength had returned quietly, without effort. Tears filled my eyes, not from exhaustion or frustration, but from gratitude. It felt like the moment when a long-carried weight finally slips from the shoulders and the body can stand upright again.

In that stillness, a scripture rose gently within my heart, carrying comfort and certainty. Psalm 27:13 (NIV) says, "I remain confident of this: I will see the goodness of the Lord in the land of the living." Those words came alive in my spirit. They did not feel like a verse written centuries ago, they felt like a personal promise spoken directly into my chest. I understood then that everything God begins, He completes, and that nothing He establishes can be overturned.

I walked to the window and looked out into the quiet darkness, watching the faint glow of distant lights across the horizon. Something in the atmosphere felt different, steady and strong, as if heaven had shifted something permanently. Instead of uncertainty, I felt understanding. Instead of hoping for possibility, I felt anchored. What once seemed distant now felt close enough to touch.

I realized that the promise was no longer something I was waiting to witness; it was something already unfolding beneath the surface, waiting only for the appointed moment to rise. The future no longer felt heavy. It felt near. It felt prepared. It felt established. What had once required constant strength now required only trust.

Sitting in the quiet, I whispered a prayer of commitment, promising

God that I would steward this calling with honor, protect it with diligence, and carry it with humility. I promised to remain faithful no matter the sacrifice, no matter the demands, and no matter the challenges that would inevitably come. I promised never to treat this vision casually, never to forget the pain that produced strength, and never to lose sight of the purpose behind the work.

I knew without question that many lives would one day walk onto that ground seeking hope, healing, and restoration. I knew that families would step through doors weighed down by pain and leave clothed in peace. I knew that futures would be rewritten and generations changed. I understood then why the path had been so difficult: anything designed to transform lives requires endurance, and anything intended to carry the weight of legacy requires depth that cannot be built quickly.

By the time I finally rested my hands in my lap, something sacred settled inside me. I no longer wondered whether the vision would come to pass. I simply looked forward to the moment God would reveal the final piece. It felt like the end of one season and the quiet beginning of another.

The internal construction was complete. The foundation within my spirit now stood firm, steady, and prepared to carry what comes next. For the first time, I did not feel like someone waiting for a door to open. I felt like someone already standing inside the threshold, watching the handle turn.

There was no rush, no anxiety, and no urgency to force movement. Strength returned in ways impossible to explain. Thoughts cleared. Breathing slowed. The turmoil that once filled nights with tension now dissolved into peace so steadily it felt like an anchor settling into place.

During that time, I became acutely aware of how much I had been transformed internally throughout the journey. The struggle had reshaped perspective, the silence had deepened conviction, and the pressure had carved a strength that could not have been built in comfort. The vision no longer felt like something I was trying to hold together with my own hands.

It felt carried. It felt protected. It felt guided by something far greater than strategy or determination. Every part of me understood that the weight was no longer mine to lift. The battle that had once consumed my energy now felt complete, even though the physical manifestation had not yet appeared. I knew, without needing proof, that the promise was already unfolding.

Even people around me could sense the change, though they knew nothing of the details. Conversations carried hope instead of concern. Support replaced hesitation. Encouragement replaced analysis. It was as if hearts began moving together under one rhythm, unified by anticipation instead of pressure.

The tone shifted from endurance to expectation. Even without documents or signatures, there was an unspoken knowing that the turning point had already arrived. What once felt heavy and uncertain now rested like a foundation wide enough to build on without fear of collapse.

The struggle had shaped discipline, forging a resolve that would not easily be swayed. The delays had sharpened discernment, allowing for a clarity of vision that had not previously existed.

The silence had built trust, a trust not based on circumstances, but on the unshakeable promise of God. The pressure had strengthened endurance, enabling me to carry the weight of the blessing to come. The waiting had refined focus, stripping away distractions and revealing the true essence of the vision.

Without those layers, the blessing would have been too heavy to carry, too overwhelming to manage. The real miracle was not the land, but the development of the person required to steward what was coming. The transformation was not about acquiring a piece of property, but about becoming the leader capable of carrying the promise into reality.

It was the cultivation of a heart that could be trusted with the responsibility of stewarding the blessing. The true breakthrough was the realization that the journey, with all its challenges and setbacks, had been preparing me for the moment when the promise would manifest.

Nothing about the journey felt unfinished anymore. The questions that once demanded answers lost their power. The fears that once whispered failure fell silent. The doubt that once clouded direction evaporated in the presence of a certainty that could no longer be shaken. The future felt real, close, and alive.

The ground that had once existed only in vision now felt like a physical reality approaching step by step. I knew with absolute conviction that the time of wandering had ended. The season of searching had fulfilled its purpose. The next step would not be about hoping. It would be about stepping forward to claim what had already been prepared.

The transition was complete, not externally, but internally. The promise was no longer a distant possibility. It was a present reality, waiting for the right moment to be revealed. The journey had shifted from fighting to receiving, from enduring to advancing, from holding on to walking into fulfillment. Everything inside me understood that what was coming next would change everything. And when the door opened, I would be ready.

CHAPTER 19

THE DAY EVERYTHING SHIFTED

The day everything shifted did not arrive with thunder or sudden clarity. It began like any other morning, quietly, without ceremony, the kind of day that could have easily blended into all the ones before it. Yet beneath that ordinary surface, something felt different. The air carried weight, not oppressive, but serious, as if the world itself paused in anticipation.

There was no announcement, no dramatic sign, just a quiet knowing that could not be ignored. The journey had reached the point where remaining in planning was no longer possible. Waiting had served its purpose. The season of questioning had done its work. Now a real decision had to be made. Not another outline, not another conversation, not another round of research. A decision with real consequences, one that would either move the vision forward or leave it locked in the safety of intention.

For days leading up to that moment, my mind wrestled with a single truth: faith must eventually leave the comfort of thought and step into action. I felt the edges of that truth pressing against my spirit each time I reviewed documents, stared at the numbers, or walked past the same stacks of papers that represented both possibility and risk.

It would have been easier to keep researching, easier to keep adjusting details, easier to remain in the phase where everything was flexible, theoretical, and safe. Planning can become a hiding place when fear resists commitment. I knew that staying there too long would eventually become disobedience. The vision had matured past preparation. It was time to decide. The question was no longer whether the assignment was real. The question was whether I would step fully into it.

That day, I sat alone at the table, surrounded by the same documents that had worn me down so many nights before. Contracts, projections, legal notes, written questions from advisors, land descriptions, cost outlines, and risks were scattered before me. Nothing was new. Every number and sentence had been reviewed so many times that I could recite them in my mind without looking.

Yet this time, the weight felt different. There was no frantic energy, no desperate attempt to find one more piece of information to make the decision easier. There was only silence, and a quiet awareness that the answer would not come from another meeting, another spreadsheet, or another voice. The decision had to come from obedience. I realized then that I was not choosing between land and no land. I was choosing between stepping into everything God had been shaping or retreating into a safety that would never satisfy my spirit again.

The emotional pressure rose slowly as I looked at everything spread before me. I thought about the years of preparation, the sacrifices, the moments when giving up almost felt reasonable, the spiritual battles that nearly broke me, the nights I wondered if I had misunderstood the assignment. I could see the faces of children in my mind, the ones I had not met yet but already carried in my heart. I could feel the longing of families who had been waiting for a place that treated their suffering with dignity.

I could hear the quiet prayers that had been lifted long before my name ever entered this story. Those images stood in the room with me more clearly than the papers on the table. The decision no longer felt like a financial commitment alone. It felt like a response to all that unseen expectation. Saying yes meant stepping fully into what God had been preparing. Saying no meant surrendering the assignment back to fear.

For a few moments, I let myself feel the full weight of what could go wrong. The possibilities came quickly. What if the resources did not arrive as I believed they would? What if unexpected issues appeared after the commitment? What if I misjudged the timing? What if those who believed alongside me felt disappointed? Those questions moved like a storm through my thoughts, each one trying to convince me that it would be wiser to wait just a little longer.

But beneath all those scenarios lived another, stronger question: What if this was the moment heaven had been preparing all along? What if delaying now was not wisdom, but disobedience dressed as caution? What if the very fear that seemed reasonable was the barrier standing between the promise and its fulfillment? That realization began to separate hesitation from discernment. Discernment protects purpose. Fear tries to paralyze it.

The turning point came when I understood that the real risk was not in moving forward, but in choosing to stay where I was. Remaining in the comfort of planning would preserve the illusion of safety, but it would also guarantee that the vision stayed stuck in theory. Every story that had ever moved me, every testimony that had reminded me of God's faithfulness, every life changed by courage had one thing in common: someone eventually decided to step without knowing how everything would unfold. Not recklessly, but obediently. Not carelessly, but surrendered.

I thought about how long this assignment had pursued me. It had followed me when I tried to rest. It had stood in the background of every other project. It had refused to let go even when I tried to quiet it. That kind of calling is not casual. It is not seasonal. It is not a passing idea. It is a divine responsibility that will not rest until it is answered.

A stillness settled over me that did not come from exhaustion. It came from clarity. The fear did not vanish completely, but it lost its authority. I understood that if I waited for a moment when every doubt disappeared, I would never move. Instead of asking for guarantees, I began asking a different question: Am I willing to trust God beyond what I can control? That question stripped everything back to its core.

The clinic, the land, the numbers, the processes, all of it mattered deeply, but none of it was the foundation of my yes. My yes had to rest on who God is, not on how secure everything felt. I realized that this chapter of the journey was not about displaying confidence to others. It was about surrendering fear privately and choosing obedience even if my voice still trembled.

The decision itself was simple in action, even though it had taken years to reach in spirit. It came down to one phone call and one message of confirmation that would move everything into motion. There was no dramatic scene. There was no audience. I picked up my phone and stared at the screen for a long moment, fully aware that pressing a single button would begin the next stage of this journey in a way that could not be reversed.

My heart was beating hard enough that I could feel it in my throat, but my hands were steady. I dialed the number and waited as the tone rang in my ear. Each second felt longer than it should have, as if time itself understood that something sacred was unfolding. When the call connected and the familiar voice answered, I spoke the words I had rehearsed many times in my mind but had never had the courage to release.

This is it. We are moving forward. I am ready to commit.

The conversation that followed did not erupt with excitement. It unfolded with calm clarity. We discussed next steps, the formalities, the written confirmation required, the structure that would follow. Every sentence carried weight, yet there was a subtle lightness in the air. The heaviness of indecision lifted with each word confirming commitment. I realized then that the hardest part had never been logistics.

The hardest part had been crossing the invisible line between almost and yes. When the call ended, I remained still for several minutes, listening to the silence that followed. It was not the same silence that had haunted previous seasons, heavy with questions and uncertainty. This silence was full. It felt like standing in a room that heaven had just entered.

After the call, I wrote the formal response that would document what my heart had already decided. It was simple, a few lines carrying the weight of everything this journey represented. As I typed, every moment that had led to this point came to mind:

The early days when the clinic was only a thought.
The nights of research when everything felt impossible.
The warfare that tried to tear the assignment apart.
The tears that fell when I felt too weak to continue.
The quiet strength that rose each time I thought of the lives this would one day touch.

All of it was contained in that moment without needing to be written. When I pressed send, there was no sudden surge of emotion, just a deep, grounded sense that something irreversible had taken place. A door had closed behind me, leaving no path back into the safety of uncertainty.

I knew then that God had carried this vision longer than I had. I knew nothing about this decision had been rushed. I knew every delay had refined, not destroyed, the assignment. I knew my yes did not rest on my ability to control outcomes but on my willingness to obey. That understanding did not erase vulnerability, but it made clear that vulnerability was no longer a reason to retreat. It was proof that I had arrived in a place where faith, not fear, must lead.

Late that night, I sat alone again. The documents on the table were the same. The numbers had not changed. The challenges had not disappeared. Yet the room no longer felt like a place of wrestling. It felt like a place of agreement. The vision no longer argued with hesitation. It had taken its rightful place at the center of everything.

I knew the road forward would still demand much. There would be more obstacles, more decisions, more moments where courage would be tested. But the most important shift had already occurred, a transformation that went beyond circumstances and rooted itself deep in conviction. The assignment was no longer something I was considering. It was something I had fully embraced, a mantle I had taken up with resolve and purpose. The weight I carried no longer felt like a question. It felt like a calling that had finally been answered in full, a responsibility I was no longer hesitant to own.

Thinking about the future that night, I did not see every detail clearly, but one thing was unmistakable: there would come a day when children would walk onto that land and receive care, when families would exhale relief after years of suffering, when people would stand on that soil and give thanks for a place that treated their pain with honor.

On that day, it would not be the paperwork that came to mind. It would be this day, the day everything shifted quietly in a room where no one was watching, the day fear lost its grip and obedience took its place, the day the journey stepped into a new chapter not because everything made sense, but because God had been faithful every step of the way.

That day did not end with celebration or applause. It ended with a calm that felt almost unfamiliar. I went to sleep knowing that tomorrow might not look different on the surface, but everything had changed beneath it. The decision had been made. The motion could not be undone. The vision had stepped from waiting into walking. And as my eyes closed, one simple truth settled deeper than any emotion: the path ahead might still be challenging, but I would not face it as someone standing outside of obedience. I would face it as someone who said yes. The next season would not be defined by questioning the calling. The next season would be about living it.

In that place of internal transformation, the truth settled deeply within me: the promise was no longer distant. It stood directly before me, preparing to unfold like a masterpiece revealed, its fulfillment imminent and inevitable. The waiting was transitioning into stepping, a deliberate and purposeful movement into the unknown, where faith and uncertainty walked hand in hand. Preparation was shifting into movement, a dynamic stride toward destiny, where every step forward became a declaration of trust and surrender.

The journey was moving from searching to claiming. I could feel the weight of the turning point even before evidence appeared. It was like standing in the doorway of a new season, hand on the handle but not yet stepping through. That moment demanded courage beyond emotion, courage rooted not in visible guarantees, but in the certainty of God's faithfulness.

One step forward would separate preparation from fulfillment. One decision would determine whether the waiting had produced strength or surrender. I knew that the next chapter required action in perfect alignment with everything God had built within me through every tear, every obstacle, and every night of silence. The time had come to step into what had been waiting.

The journey was no longer defined by struggle. It was defined by readiness. It was defined by transformation. It was defined by the quiet assurance that what once seemed impossible would soon become reality. And although the full manifestation had not yet appeared, I understood without hesitation that I stood at the edge of something extraordinary. The miracle was already breathing beneath the surface, preparing to rise. All that remained was the moment when faith stepped fully into fulfillment.

The battle had shifted. It was no longer about resistance or warfare, but about the quiet weight of responsibility pressing against the core of who I was becoming. Stepping closer to the promise required confronting fears that could no longer be ignored and releasing any reliance on personal strength. There were moments when I sat in silence, surrounded by stacks of papers, maps, and documents, staring without seeing, because the real struggle had moved from planning to believing.

The closer the miracle came, the more fiercely the mind fought to protect itself from disappointment. Hope grew heavier, not lighter, because it now carried the expectation of fulfillment. Part of me wrestled with the possibility that everything invested could collapse without warning. Thoughts tried to convince me to shrink back, to retreat, to choose safety over destiny. Yet something deeper than fear insisted that retreat was impossible. There was no turning back. The road behind me had closed. Only forward remained.

In that season, vulnerability revealed itself in ways I had never experienced. It is one thing to fight for a dream at the beginning, when excitement fuels every step. It is another thing entirely to fight for a dream when you have poured out everything you possess and the outcome remains beyond your reach. That space strips away every illusion and exposes who you are, without performance, without applause, and without visible reward. It is a refining fire that burns away pride, ego, and self-reliance.

I discovered that purpose requires standing in that fire long enough to be reshaped, refusing to escape even when escape feels reasonable. The journey forced me to ask myself questions no one else could answer. Was I willing to risk failure publicly if obedience demanded it? Was I willing to sacrifice comfort for calling? Was I willing to walk into the unknown with nothing but conviction? Those questions did not intimidate me, they transformed me. I realized that faith is not the absence of fear, but the refusal to surrender to it.

The greatest clarity came in the moments when nothing moved. In those quiet hours, when prayer felt like empty breath and progress seemed invisible, I confronted the deepest parts of my identity. I began to understand that purpose will always challenge the version of yourself too small to carry it. If the vision remained safe, it would not require transformation. If the dream remained comfortable, it would not demand growth. I felt God stretching the borders of my capacity, widening the space within me to hold more responsibility, more discipline, more resilience, and more compassion.

It was not just the land that was being prepared, it was the builder, being formed to step onto it. The fear that once whispered collapse became silent. The anxiety that pressed against my chest loosened its grip. The sense of being overwhelmed transformed into a calm that settled deeply, like steady ground beneath unsteady feet. It felt as if the weight I had carried alone for so long had been lifted, replaced with a strength that could not be explained through reason.

I recognized that God had not merely answered prayer. He had strengthened the vessel receiving the answer. The storm that once felt endless had served its purpose. It had built something inside me that no amount of teaching or strategy could have produced. It had built endurance. It had built depth. It had built the capacity to walk into the fulfillment of the vision without trembling.

Every tear, every obstacle, every delay, every night of silence, every moment of confusion, every closed door, and every sacrifice had shaped the leader required to carry what was coming. Without the pressure, I would not have discovered the strength waiting beneath the surface. Without the struggle, I would not have developed the clarity needed to navigate what lay ahead. Without waiting, I would not have grown into the person capable of stewarding the promise with maturity instead of emotion. The journey had become a divine tool, shaping character, sharpening faith, and sculpting identity into alignment with purpose.

What once felt distant now stands near. What once felt fragile now stands unshakeable. What once belonged to imagination now stands ready to transition into reality. The waiting has fulfilled its purpose. The internal construction is complete. The time has come to move from preparation into possession. The next step will carry the weight of destiny.

CHAPTER 20

REFLECTION: WHEN THE DUST SETTLES

I never understood the cost of purpose until I walked through valleys that tested every part of my spirit. I never understood the power of endurance until I faced days when quitting felt easier than standing. I never understood the depth of faith until silence replaced answers and I had nothing left to hold except God Himself. There were nights when the only prayer I could form was a whisper, when the strength to speak felt beyond reach, and when exhaustion drowned every other emotion.

Yet even in the stillness of those moments, God did not release His grip. He did not step back. He did not abandon or ignore. Instead, He stayed close enough to breathe strength into the places that had run empty. His presence spoke louder than His silence. His nearness carried more power than the answers I thought I needed. Psalm 34:18 (NIV) declares, "The Lord is close to the brokenhearted and saves those who are crushed in spirit." I learned what that truly means. He drew near, not to rescue me from the fight, but to teach me how to stand inside it.

Looking back now, I see how every struggle carved something valuable into my soul. I see how pressure stripped away dependence on human ability and replaced it with dependence on His voice. I see how weakness became a doorway to humility, and humility became the foundation of strength. I see how surrender replaced striving, and peace replaced panic.

I see how the storm that felt endless was shaping the strength required for what is coming. Every setback forged courage. Every disappointment sharpened my vision. Every closed door directed the path with more accuracy than success ever could. The journey did not harden me, it humbled me. It did not break my faith, it purified it. It did not weaken my spirit, it made me unshakable.

There is a part of the journey that no one else can witness: the place where tears fall quietly in rooms where no audience is present and no applause follows. It is in that hidden place where character is formed. It is in that hidden place where the soul is refined. It is in that hidden place where God reveals that purpose is not built in victory, but in vulnerability. If I had never walked through the silence, I would not know the sound of God's whisper. If I had never faced fear, I would not know the strength of courage. If I had never reached the point of feeling empty, I would not know that He alone is enough. What once looked like painful waiting now appears as sacred preparation.

When I reflect on the road already traveled, I finally understand why God did not reveal the ending from the beginning. If He had shown me the full weight of the journey before it began, I might have walked away in fear. If He had exposed every battle in advance, I might have chosen a safer path. Instead, He allowed each step to unfold one at a time, giving only enough light to take the next step in front of me.

Faith was never meant to see the entire road. Faith was designed to trust the One who does. And I have learned something that will stay with me for the rest of my life: God does not explain Himself before He moves. He reveals Himself once you trust Him enough to keep walking.

Now, standing at the threshold of promise, I feel something deeper than celebration or relief. I feel gratitude, a steady, profound gratitude that reaches into the quiet corners of my soul. I am grateful for the nights that forced me to pray from the core of my being. I am grateful for the days when all I could do was stand still and breathe. I am grateful for every tear shed in silence that watered endurance. I am grateful for every delay that protected the vision. I am grateful for every battle that built strength. I am grateful for a God who does not rush His work simply to satisfy our desire for speed. I am grateful for a God who finishes what He begins.

He was shaping capacity. He was strengthening the foundation beneath the assignment. He was removing the pieces that could not carry the weight of destiny. The most painful chapters became the most necessary, because they formed the ability to stand under pressure without folding. They forged endurance that cannot be taught through ease. They formed spiritual muscles that could not be strengthened through simplicity.

I discovered why Scripture declares in James 1:4 (NIV) that "perseverance must finish its work so that you may be mature and complete, not lacking anything." That verse became truth embodied, not words printed. Perseverance built the structure inside me that purpose required outside of me.

It proves that faith is not a feeling; it is a decision. A decision to believe when belief hurts. A decision to continue when continuing feels impossible. A decision to hold onto what God spoke even when reality contradicts every part of it. I realized then that the journey had never been about land, or paperwork, or logistics. It had been about becoming someone who could carry destiny without destroying it and without being destroyed by it.

Reflection forced me to confront truths about myself that I could not have learned through ease. I confronted my impatience. I confronted my desire for control. I confronted the parts of myself that clung to timelines and feared uncertainty. I confronted identity rooted in performance rather than surrender. In the quiet, God stripped away the illusion that strength comes from self-reliance and replaced it with a deeper revelation: true strength is found only in dependence upon Him.

I learned that leadership is not proven by how loudly you can speak, but by how humbly you can listen. Not by how boldly you move in public, but by how steadfastly you stand when no one is watching. Not by how confidently you inspire others, but by how faithfully you obey when obedience costs everything. The journey did not teach me simply how to build. It taught me how to kneel. It taught me how to trust. It taught me how to surrender.

As reflection settled deeper, I began to understand something crucial: every person will face a season where life demands a fight they never asked for. A fight for identity. A fight for purpose. A fight for sanity. A fight for faith. A fight for family. A fight that pushes the heart past its limits and stretches the soul beyond its comfort. In those moments, quitting will feel easier than continuing, and silence will feel louder than prayer. It is in those moments that people must discover what they truly believe.

I want every person who reads this to know that endurance is not reserved for the strong. It is built through weakness. Strength is not born through winning. It is built through surviving. Faith is not proven by certainty. It is proven by persistence. The battle will not break you if you refuse to bow to it. The pain will not defeat you if you refuse to surrender. You do not need to see the finish line to keep moving toward it. Sometimes the greatest victory is taking the next step when every part of you is telling you to stop.

Looking back now, I am grateful for everything I once prayed God would remove. I am grateful for every unanswered prayer, every closed door, every disappointment, and every silent night. They did not come to punish me. They came to train me. They did not come to delay destiny. They came to prepare me to carry it. The weight that once felt unbearable now reveals itself as the weight that built my foundation.

And standing in this place of reflection, I no longer ask why the journey hurt. I now understand that without the pain, purpose would have remained fragile. Without the struggle, faith would have stayed shallow. Without the pressure, capacity would have stayed small. The journey broke what needed to break and rebuilt what needed to stand.

As I step forward from this season into what comes next, I carry the assurance that nothing endured was wasted. Not a tear. Not a prayer. Not a sacrifice. Not a silent night. Every moment was preparation for the miracle that is now closer than breath. The land is no longer a dream or a distant hope. It is a promise waiting for completion, a reality approaching with unshakeable certainty.

Standing on the threshold of fulfillment, I take a deep breath and allow the weight of gratitude to settle over every part of my spirit. I am not the same person I was when this journey began. I have been rebuilt

The person who began this fight years ago is not the same person writing these words now. The earlier version of me carried passion but lacked the endurance required for responsibility on this scale. That version of me wanted answers quickly, expected progress instantly, and assumed faith would remove pressure. Experience taught something different. Faith does not remove pressure; it prepares you to endure it. Endurance matures commitment. Pain shapes capacity. Waiting reveals discipline. And struggle builds the kind of foundation that cannot be shaken by circumstance or opinion.

The process shaped the kind of leader required to carry long-term responsibility. It developed resilience necessary not only for the purchase of the land, but for every stage of construction, operation, and expansion that will follow. The journey demanded growth that could not be gained from theory or inspiration; it required experience, pressure, sacrifice, and consistency.

Standing here now, the weight I feel is not the weight of exhaustion, but the weight of assignment. It is the weight of understanding that the work ahead will impact lives far beyond my lifetime. It will shape futures, restore dignity, and rewrite stories long after my name is no longer mentioned. That realization changes everything. It shifts motivation from personal success to generational responsibility. Purpose is no longer something imagined. It has become something that must be built carefully and stewarded with integrity.

Looking ahead brings clarity to what this moment truly represents. It is not the conclusion of a dream. It is the doorway into execution. The season that once demanded waiting now demands action. The pages that follow this chapter will not be about searching or learning how to endure. They will be about building something designed to withstand time and serve communities who have waited far too long for accessible healing and support.

The responsibility is no longer to prove that the vision is possible, but to protect and develop it with discipline and strategy. There is a deep awareness that every decision made from this point forward must be intentional, measured, and aligned with long-term sustainability. What is built must outlive emotion and personal energy. It must be designed to stand independently, strong enough to succeed without relying on a single individual.

Nothing about the future feels uncertain anymore. The work ahead carries challenges, but none of the uncertainty that once clouded the beginning. The battles that tested endurance have already proven that purpose cannot be destroyed by delay or resistance.

The process revealed which voices matter and which distractions must be left behind. It confirmed that vision is strongest when built slowly, honestly, and with accountability. It exposed weaknesses that needed to be strengthened and revealed strengths that needed to be trusted. This season brought a maturity that removes the need for validation and replaces it with quiet conviction. The calling is now clearer than ever: build something that cannot be undone by time, opposition, or circumstance.

More than anything, there is deep gratitude for every struggle that shaped this moment. The hardest seasons produced the most significant growth. The nights of silence built discipline. The delays protected direction. The pressure forged character. The battles clarified identity. Nothing was wasted. Not a single step.

And now, standing between what has been and what is about to begin, it becomes evident that the journey was never about proving a dream could become reality. It was about becoming the person capable of carrying the responsibility that reality will require. The mission has reached a place where personal strength is no longer the foundation. The purpose is. Responsibility is. Legacy is.

The vision now extends far beyond the groundbreaking moment. It stretches into the future where doors will open to families seeking care, where children will walk into a place built to protect their dignity, where lives will be changed not by speeches or promises, but by access to real help.

This is the beginning of something that will shape generations and reshape a community. It is the start of work that will continue long after this chapter is closed. There is no turning back. There is no room for hesitation. There is no space for fear. The time ahead is now about building, protecting, expanding, and preparing others to one day carry the mission further than I ever could.

The land will be secured in its appointed time. The foundation will be laid with intention and care. The walls will rise as a testimony to endurance. The doors will open not as a surprise, but as the visible confirmation of a promise that survived every obstacle and every season of doubt, finally standing before those who once wondered if it would ever come to pass.

What followed was not excitement, but sobriety. The realization settled that the work ahead would demand more discipline than inspiration and more structure than emotion. Vision had already been proven. What remained was responsibility. The season ahead would require decisions that favored longevity over speed, wisdom over impulse, and stewardship over urgency.

I understood then that carrying purpose forward would require a different kind of strength than surviving the journey that brought me here. Endurance had built resilience, but leadership would now demand consistency. Faith would no longer be exercised primarily through waiting, but through execution. Every step forward would require discernment grounded in accountability rather than emotion.

This was the moment where preparation transitioned into obligation. The calling was no longer forming. It was operational. What had been nurtured privately would now be tested publicly. The work ahead would require systems, safeguards, partnerships, and decisions that protected the mission beyond my presence. The purpose was no longer personal; it was communal.

I recognized that building something meant to last required resisting the temptation to rush. Speed could create movement, but only structure could sustain impact. The future demanded patience applied strategically, faith expressed practically, and vision guarded carefully. The assignment was no longer to prove belief, but to steward what belief had already secured.

This was not the beginning of another waiting season. It was the beginning of intentional construction. The ground had already been prepared. What followed would determine how firmly what was built could stand long after the initial momentum passed.

In the quiet places where no applause exists, character is built. Motivation can collapse under pressure, but conviction is born in pressure. Strength does not appear at the end of the journey. It is formed in the middle. It is the unglamorous, unseen, uncelebrated work that produces what the world eventually calls miraculous.

No one watching from the outside truly understands the weight that had to be carried, the nights spent wrestling with doubt, or the internal battles fought in solitude. Yet those hidden moments built the foundation that nothing visible will ever shake. The parts of the story no one witnessed became the reason the visible testimony stands unbreakable.

Now, standing in this space between what has been endured and what is about to be revealed, the meaning becomes unmistakably clear. Strength was never the result of success. Strength was the result of refusing to collapse. Vision lived because surrender was not an option.

Hope survived because it learned to breathe even when oxygen felt scarce. Courage was formed not in moments of applause, but in moments of isolation where the only voice available to trust was God's. The greatest victory was not securing land. The greatest victory was becoming the person who could carry it without breaking.

That weight demands honesty. It demands courage. It demands a willingness to continue even when the body trembles, the mind aches, and the heart feels worn thin. Yet the miracle is found in the realization that the strength to continue does not originate from within. It rises from the space where surrender meets resilience, where dependence meets divine reinforcement, and where humility meets supernatural empowerment. The battle reveals that endurance is not a trait; it is a transformation. It turns the ordinary into the unbreakable and the fragile into the fortified. It turns wounds into wisdom and weakness into authority.

The pressure that feels relentless is not working against you; it is working within you. It is shaping the character required to carry what is coming. If the road feels heavy, it is because you are carrying something weighty enough to change lives. If the journey feels long, it is because the impact will stretch farther than you can currently imagine.

Do not measure your progress by visible results; measure it by the fact that you are still standing. The enemy does not fight empty hands. He fights future impact. The warfare around you is evidence that something powerful is moving toward you, and the fact that you have not collapsed is proof that you are stronger than you ever realized. Keep breathing. Keep stepping. Keep believing. The ground beneath your feet is shifting, even if your eyes cannot yet perceive it.

And now, as this chapter approaches the quiet doorway of transition, something sacred rises within the silence. The weight feels different. The air is lighter. The horizon looks clearer. The promise that once seemed distant now rests close enough to touch, not as an idea, but as a reality waiting for its appointed unveiling. The strength built through struggle stands like a pillar beneath my soul, supporting every breath with confidence rather than uncertainty.

The evidence of growth and transformation is already present, manifesting in quiet yet profound ways. The weight of responsibility remains, but it no longer feels overwhelming or unstable. It has become a manageable, integral part of who I am. The air feels lighter, the horizon clearer, and the promise that once seemed distant is unfolding steadily, moving toward its appointed moment with certainty and purpose.

The strength forged in the fire of pressure has become a foundation within me, steady and enduring, allowing me to navigate the uncertainties of the future with assurance. I am not rushing what lies ahead. I am allowing it to unfold, trusting that every step, every trial, and every triumph has been leading me to this moment of clarity and understanding.

Hope now stands firm and unshakeable, a beacon of light shaped by faith tested, refined, and proven steady. Faith stands without trembling. Vision stretches forward unobstructed, clear and purposeful. What once felt fragile has taken root. I understand now that the journey was never about reaching an ending. It was about becoming prepared to carry what comes next, about becoming the person God created me to be, about becoming the vessel capable of holding the promise, and about becoming the instrument through which purpose is fulfilled.

www.ingramcontent.com/pod-product-compliance
Lightning Source LLC
Chambersburg PA
CBHW030410130626
46549CB00004B/1712